LITERACY & LIBRARIES
Learning from Case Studies

GraceAnne A. DeCandido, Editor

Prof 021 Literacy

OFFICE FOR LITERACY AND OUTREACH SERVICES
AMERICAN LIBRARY ASSOCIATION

Chicago and London

2001

Cover by Tessing Design

Text design by Dianne M. Rooney

Composition by ALA Editions using QuarkXpress 4.1 for the PC, with Minion and Helvetica Condensed typefaces.

The paper used in this publication meets the minimum requirements of American National Standard for Information Sciences—Permanence of Paper for Printed Library Materials, ANSI Z39.48-1992. ∞

Library of Congress Cataloging-in-Publication Data

Literacy and libraries : learning from case studies / GraceAnne A. DeCandido, editor.
    p.   cm.
  ISBN 0-8389-3516-8
    1. Libraries and new literates—United States—Case studies. 2. Public libraries—Services to illiterate persons—United States—Case studies. 3. Literacy programs—United States—Case studies. I. DeCandido, GraceAnne A.
Z716.45 .L58 2001
021.2′4′0973—dc21
                                                      2001022439

Printed in the United States of America

05 04 03 02 01   5 4 3 2 1

■ CONTENTS ■

PART III ■ LITERACY AND TECHNOLOGY

■ ACKNOWLEDGMENTS ■

Many individuals and organizations contributed to the compilation, writing, and publication of this volume. A large measure of thanks goes to the 13 library literacy programs that made up the first phase of the Literacy in Libraries Across America (LILAA) Initiative funded by the Lila Wallace-Reader's Digest Fund and the American Library Association.

The literacy program directors, literacy teachers, librarians, library directors, and adult learners from these 13 library literacy programs were accustomed to being trailblazers, standard bearers, and champions for library literacy. During the course of this initiative, they valiantly accepted many challenges and numerous responsibilities. A major responsibility was to tell, with passion, determination, and data, the story of adult literacy in their library and community. They have successfully completed that responsibility and the proof of their success is in the following chapters.

In an effort to tell a good and true story, we collected contributions from technology consultants, researchers, and ALA directors. Their voices provide a broader context for library literacy, demonstrate the far-reaching impact of the LILAA Initiative, and enrich the story. Thank you for contributing your expertise and energy!

The book's editor, GraceAnne DeCandido, demonstrated a remarkable skill. Early on in this process, she envisioned the individual stories and contributions as a real book. Throughout, GraceAnne was a supportive presence, a knowledgeable librarian, and a remarkably graceful editor.

Finally, thanks to the Lila Wallace-Reader's Digest Fund for its substantial economic investment and deep belief in public libraries, adult literacy, and the American Library Association. In addition to financially supporting ALA and library literacy programs, the Lila Wallace-Reader's Digest Fund committed enormous time, energy, and passion to libraries and adult literacy. Thanks to the LILAA Initiative and the Fund, library literacy programs and ALA have claimed a powerful and respected voice in the adult literacy field. For that, we are deeply grateful.

During the final years of the LILAA Initiative, the Lila Wallace-Reader's Digest Fund developed and funded research initiatives to demonstrate the impact of literacy in libraries. The survey, *Literacy Programs for Adults in Public Libraries,* conducted by the Library Research Center, Graduate School of Library and Information Science at the University of Illinois, provides current and reliable information about the number of libraries providing adult literacy services and their needs for the future. This survey data help tell the story of literacy in libraries with numbers and narratives. The results of the survey and other research initiatives will have a lasting effect on the adult education, literacy, and language system.

We hope that this volume will inform the adult literacy field about the significant role that libraries play in the adult education system. In addition, we sincerely hope that this volume will mentor a new generation of library literacy advocates, instructors, librarians, policy makers, educators, and public officials—a new generation with a vision for the future that includes libraries and literacy for all!

Throughout this volume, we have included excerpts from *Literacy Programs for Adults in Public Libraries,* a survey report prepared for the Lila Wallace-Reader's Digest Fund by Leigh Estabrook and Edward Lakner, the Library Research Center, Graduate School of Library and Information Science, University of Illinois, January 2000.

We include the following executive summary from the report, and the excerpts are indicated in shaded boxes throughout the text.

Executive Summary: This report presents the findings from a national survey of literacy programs for adults in public libraries, to assess the role of public libraries in providing learning opportunities for adults to improve their literacy skills. Data were collected regarding the range of adult literacy activities in libraries, types of partnerships in which libraries are involved, forms of participation and instruction, and the factors that explain library involvement in literacy instruction. The Library Research Center (LRC) of the University of Illinois conducted the study with funding from the Lila Wallace-Reader's Digest Fund (LWRD). All public libraries serving from 5,000 to 100,000 or more patrons received the questionnaire. Libraries serving populations between 5,000 and 99,999 were sampled if they met certain criteria regarding staff size, hours open, and annual operating expenditures. There were 1,067 completed questionnaires for a response rate of 72.7%.

DALE PHILLIPS LIPSCHULTZ

■ INTRODUCTION ■

The institutions, programs, and individuals featured in this book demonstrate the many ways in which libraries and adult literacy programs change lives. This book is about a very special learning community. This community is grown in the public library, an institution dedicated to providing equity of access to all. Roles are released, relished, and frequently reversed here. In each chapter, researchers, library directors, program administrators, teachers, tutors, and librarians become learners, while adult learners share what they've learned and become literacy leaders.

Each author graciously contributed his or her unique story. Throughout the book, adult learners contributed their words and experiences. Now combined, these individual stories provide a chapter-by-chapter report on the state of adult literacy in libraries. As a caveat, some of the names of adult learners have been changed to protect their privacy, while other names are boldly inscribed. Both approaches demonstrate the power and permanence of the printed word.

The book is organized into four parts. The first section, *Literacy Now*, provides an empirical framework for examining adult literacy in libraries. In chapter 1, Sondra Cuban uses Gloria's story to weave together culture, history, and literacy. This powerful narrative helps us understand the hopes, dreams, and disappointments of adult learners. In addition, this chapter establishes the essential role of library literacy programs in adult education. In chapter 2, researchers from the National Center for the Study of Adult Learning and Literacy (NCSALL) and the Manpower Demonstration Research Corporation (MDRC) describe a research project addressing the complex issues of learner participation and persistence. Adult learners in five library literacy programs "share their worlds" with researchers in an effort to improve program practices, make programs more accessible to adult learners, and further explore the role that libraries play in adult education.

In chapter 3, Leslie McGinnis, Second Start Adult Literacy Program, Oakland (Calif.) Public Library, reflects upon and shares the challenges, successes, and lessons learned as a result of Second Start's journey toward participatory education and a truly learner-centered library literacy program. In chapter 4, Sherry Drobner introduces us to "ordinary" heroes as she describes the "Students Be Tutors" program at Alameda County Public Library. In this context, adult learners created new teaching models by "appropriating the role of the teacher and reconstructing the teaching of literacy skills." In chapter 5, Taylor Willingham, Santa Clara County (Calif.) Public Library, illustrates how learner involvement significantly benefits and challenges library literacy programs.

The second section of the book, *How We Do What We Do*, features the voices and stories of library directors, literacy program directors, and program staff. Taken together, their stories create a panorama of library literacy programs in large and small libraries, in urban centers and rural communities, meeting the educational needs of English-language speakers and speakers of other languages.

In chapter 6, Dinah O'Brien challenges the traditional and dearly held assumption that everyone over the age of 10 can read English on at least the fifth-grade level. The chapter describes how the Plymouth (Mass.) Public Library developed literacy strategies and programs that are fully integrated into the mission and mainstream of the library. In chapter 7, Lynne Price uses stories to provide a snapshot of library literacy at Project READ, San Francisco (Calif.) Public Library. First, the chapter details Project READ's use of portfolio assessment and periodic interviews to document the learner progress. Then, the story of a learner-tutor pair brings the teaching, learning, and assessment process to life.

In chapter 8, Kathy Endaya, Project READ, Redwood City, California, illustrates how a city in the heart of Silicon Valley used its community's needs and opportunities to guide the development and implementation of literacy programs providing services for adults, families, and children. In chapter 9, Konni Clayton, Robinson Township (Ill.) Public Library, tells the story of how one rural public library in east central Illinois started and sustained an adult literacy program. In chapter 10, Decklan Fox, New York Public Library's Centers for Reading and Writing, examines and describes the process used to develop two essential literacy program components: instruction and curriculum. In chapter 11, Bruce Carmel and Anita Citron, Queens Borough (N.Y.) Public Library, eloquently illustrate why there are no simple answers to frequently asked questions (FAQs) about program identity, student population, and instructional methodology. Their response to these FAQs offers insight into the ways in which the adult literacy programs at Queens Borough Public Library provide quality literacy instruction to a diverse student population.

In chapter 12, Steve Sumerford, Greensboro (N.C.) Public Library, urges "libraries and librarians to reclaim literacy as an issue that is at the very heart and soul of our institutions" in an effort to lead the fight against functional illiteracy. The author uses three powerful examples to illustrate how libraries can contribute to this effort. In chapter 13, Lou Sua, Greensboro (N.C.) Public Library, demonstrates how, on a community level, libraries and literacy are destined to travel hand-in-hand. As a librarian, the author sees herself as a "facilitator of learning." Throughout the chapter she describes her efforts to develop programs that address the complex needs of individuals who are not traditional library patrons. Gary Strong, Queens Borough (N.Y.) Public Library, contributed the final chapter in this section. Using the words of adult learners, the author tells a poignant story of humiliation, hope, and worlds made possible by learning to read and write at "the people's university."

The third section of the book, *Literacy and Technology,* explores the integration of technology into new and existing library literacy programs. In chapter 15, authors Sarah Nixon and Tim Ponder articulate the sociocultural theory of human development that guides most library literacy programs. From this perspective, the authors view the integration and use of technology as a profoundly social process, just like learning to read and write.

In chapter 16, Susan O'Connor and Debbie Guerra, Brooklyn Public Library, illustrate how the acquisition of computers and application tools contributed to the development of project-based learning in Brooklyn's adult literacy programs. The authors eloquently describe how and why technology changed the way reading and writing was approached, taught, and learned. At Brooklyn Public Library, adult literacy students learn to read and write in a risk-free, collaborative, and active environment.

In chapter 17, Carol Morris, Literacy Program of Lake County, Waukegan (Ill.) Public Library, describes how computers and telecommunications technology were integrated into an existing literacy program. Initially, adult learners and literacy program staff worked together to select software and develop user-friendly "Easy In-Easy Out" guides. When the program gained access to telecommunications systems, the same collaborative strategies were used to make the Internet easily accessible.

In chapter 18, Randall Weaver, Project READ, San Francisco (Calif.) Public Library, describes how technology creates and enhances learning communities in the public library. In the best of all possible worlds, computers and telecommunications technology are skillfully and seamlessly integrated into the literacy program, becoming another learning tool in a learner-centered environment.

The final section of the book examines and explores the *History and the Future* of literacy in libraries. In chapter 19, Martín Gómez, Brooklyn (N.Y.) Public Library, notes that libraries have not always assumed and embraced the role of "literacy-centered institutions." In an effort to address and resolve this issue, the author developed a comprehensive 13-point blueprint designed to help public libraries, librarians, and communities become "literacy-centered institutions."

In chapter 20, Peggy Barber, American Library Association, urges librarians to "embrace the (literacy) issue and seize the power, satisfaction, and recognition for providing a valuable service." The author succinctly traces the history of ALA, libraries, and adult literacy. For ALA, libraries, and adult literacy, the twentieth century was indeed a century of progress and quiet achievement. The author urges the library profession and ALA to stand tall for literacy since "a literate public demands good libraries; good libraries create a literate public." In chapter 21, Satia Orange, ALA's Office for Literacy and Outreach Services, reminds us that "libraries ensure access to information for all." The author calls on ALA and America's libraries to use their significant resources to bridge the information "chasm" created by education and technology, and to provide library services to underserved populations. The book closes with GraceAnne DeCandido's 1994 editorial from *Wilson Library Bulletin* as a coda about the power of words.

Throughout the book, adult literacy is observed, implemented, and documented in the profoundly social context of the public library. The programs featured are by their own description active, project-based, learner-centered, and participatory. This is a book about barriers and bridges.

DALE PHILLIPS LIPSCHULTZ

■ 1 ■

Gloria's Story
"She Wanted Me to Be Somebody"

A Learner in a Library Literacy Program in Hawai'i

SONDRA CUBAN

And so, history goes on, written in long volumes by foreign people. Whole libraries begin to form, book upon book, shelf upon shelf. At the same time, the stories go on, generation to generation, family to family. . . . If it is truly our history Western historians desire to know, they must first put down their books, and take up our practices. First, of course, the language. But later, the people, the aina, the stories. Above all, in the end, the stories. Historians must listen, they must hear the generational connections, the reservoir of sounds and meanings.[1]

The life history of Gloria, a mid-life Hawaiian woman who is a learner in a library literacy program, is not on a public library shelf. (Her name has been changed to protect her privacy.) It is not in an archives for historians to research, nor is it in a museum for the public to see and know. The story is a bittersweet memory for this woman who shared parts of her life with me. Now it will live on in the story I am about to tell you.

I worry I cannot present Gloria more fully—as the witty woman so filled with desire and wisdom that she is. This comes after reading over numerous transcript pages from the five life story interviews I conducted with her over the course of a year.

This story comes from the author's dissertation entitled "Before Days: Women in a Library Literacy Program in Hilo, Hawai'i Talk Story" (University of Wisconsin–Madison, 1999).

As part of my doctoral research from 1997 to 1998, I interviewed her and nine other women learners in a library literacy program in Hawai'i. The interviews were open-ended and biographical. The women told me about their family learning experiences, their schooling experiences, their work histories, and their social networks. I wanted to learn more about literacy, learning, and schooling from the perspectives of both Adult Basic Education (ABE) learners and English as a Second Language (ESL) learners. Then programs could apply this knowledge and better match the needs of women in mid-life, from different cultural backgrounds. I wanted to see how literacy emerged from these experiences, rather than studying it in isolation.

I had the honor of getting to know Gloria in many different contexts apart from interviewing sessions, including visits to her home and her family's home, swimming in the ocean together, hanging out, and attending community events through her church and through the literacy program. I went to Gloria for advice about the research, to check my observations, for introductions to people, and, I have to admit, for other problems that she helped me resolve. Gloria was not just an interviewee but also an informant, a wise advisor, and a friend.

This is a story about a woman whose lifelong dream was to be "somebody." This dream, however, was often fractured when she had to face institutional demands for literacy like filling in forms, reports, and work memos. These experiences diminished her hope for her future. Yet this story reveals a woman who is resilient despite obstacles in her life.

Gloria's story, "She Wanted Me to Be Somebody," is about a dream she couldn't realize—a dream, in part, of her mother's. Gloria's mother wanted to move her daughter out of rural Kona, with its backbreaking work in coffee, to urban Honolulu in order to be self-sufficient, to be "somebody" as a beautician. Gloria tried but realized that she "can't" read and write while on the job and consequently was not hired. She talked about the freedom she experienced—from studying for the tests by memorizing and rhyming words to the independent life she led with her sister and fiancé. Finally, she realized that she could not share her literacy problems in the workplace.

From "She Wanted Me to Be Somebody"[2]

My mom wanted me to get out from the coffee field and be somebody. In our household, there were five of us so the oldest take care of the second. The second take care of the third, right. So each helping one another. My sister was [an] airline stewardess. The oldest one for Pan Am. And then she didn't . . . she stopped. Actually I call her the jack of all trade and the master of none. She's very intelligent. She can get herself into anything and do well at it. So when I went to school 'cause my mom didn't want me to stay in Hawai'i. . . . She wanted me to be somebody. To get ahead. So even knowing that I couldn't read or write, nothing was impossible. I never regretted that in me. You don't know until you try. Nothing is impossible. Oh I said, get on the board and ride it.

So I went [to] fill out the application form and my mom them . . . they didn't have that much to support me. So it was fun to step out on my own. My sister was there so I get to live with her and the school was fabulous. The reading was horrible. I still remember the word like I tell you one word, it got to do with this muscle right here—[sternocleidomastoid]. You know why I like the word—because it sounds so big and beautiful. So delicious. Makes you look so smart. It's a good thing I know what it is. It's the side of your neck muscles. . . . So I could learn to take the test. I had to rhyme them with a animal or rhyme them with something I could remember, like "oc" like ocipula is oculi. I thought of the octopus. And that's how I could remember the word. Around the eye muscle. But it was fun I enjoyed it.

It must be on two years going on three I think because the first year my mom paid for the tuition. And the second year she couldn't pay it. And my husband paid for it. My boyfriend, actually my husband-to-be. He paid for it for me 'cause he knew I wanted it and that from there, I was getting a lot better. But still in the back of my mind, I was afraid. Because you have to make ladies color in their hair. So I didn't want to make anybody bald. 'Cause those days you have to mix the formula. To give her that tone of color that she want, and now you can just walk into the store and slap it on your head. That those days you have to mix the formula—the peroxide and the coloring to make that regular color—what you come out and how long you leave it. You have to test it and sometimes you have to bleach the hair out. And if you bleach it too much, the lady will come out bald. I mean the hair is going to fall out. So that's one thing I thought of that—I was frightened. That I wasn't too happy about . . . 'cause you see I'm trying responsibility of somebody's head you know. I certainly don't want that woman to go out with green hair or being bald. And never going to work for someone else that have been sued.

So, when I had to think about that, then I had a . . . this is what I feel it, in every little boy growing up, they had a dream. And then they can't fulfill their dream because they real likely can't get to it and then you just fail. OK, I can't do it no more. Just bury it and you forget what your dream was really about. And you bury it and you don't look back. 'Cause it hurts if you have to look back to it. 'Cause you almost, you can't get to it. There's no way you can get back to where you was. 'Cause everybody has a gift. Everybody enjoy doing something but when you realize you can't get to it, because you don't have the proper help, and you never got to the right person to encourage you to give you the tool that you didn't get and excel in that area—you bury the thing that you love the most.

I told one of the girls, you know I get hard time reading and writing. Oh, because they call in and you have to take their name down. And the appointment. And I couldn't write anybody's name. And then she tell me go mix the formula in the back and I couldn't mix the formula. And this is got to do at the army base. And this is a brand new salon. And she was in a hurry. She had big clientele and that told me. That just like brought reality. And I says oh Gloria, you can't do this. This is the first time I ever use the word, can't. But when you face reality, you have to say it like it is. There's a fact here—you can't go no further for now so I told the lady, I said I have a hard time reading and writing to the process? I said I don't think I can do. I said but I won't be able to help you when it come to mix the formula or to take down notes. And I said why, 'cause I can't. And then she was very nice to me and she says well she wasn't going to hire me. So that's when I realized don't tell anybody else anymore 'cause you won't get a job.

Gloria's desire to obtain an education to fulfill this dream represents her desire to be "somebody." Her biggest obstacles were her lack of literacy skills, her lack of resources, and discrimination; she constantly told me she had "champagne tastes" but "beer money." She, like many other Hawaiians, often end up at the bottom of the economic ladder with less access to higher education.[3] Eventually, Gloria moved back to the Big Island and ended up in a literacy program for work-related and welfare reasons. Her desire to be "somebody" was also a metaphor that was rooted in her need to be publicly validated and connected to her identity. Women's identities are important to acknowledge in their return to school.[4]

What most struck me about Gloria's story was the support of her family but no one else. There seemed to be few advocates for her, as she stated, "and you never got to the right person to encourage you to give you the tool that you didn't get and excel in that area." It made me think that library literacy programs' "gift" could be to help build her supportive base by becoming proactive advocates in her life and in the lives of other learners who face outside literacy demands.

Library literacy programmers can help build a strong base of advocacy for learners in their communities by creating leadership opportunities, learning communities, curriculum that is relevant to learners' lives, and by using their resources and knowledge to advocate on their behalf

> It is not surprising that libraries have become significant providers of adult literacy instruction. Improving literacy is in the self-interest of libraries, concerned about making information, literature and culture available to all. *Survey*, p. x

Why libraries? Because they are strongly rooted in communities and can serve as institutional bridges.[5] Libraries also have many resources and access to print and electronic information sources, as well as community agencies. Libraries employ trained professionals to help people with their multiple needs. Libraries have helped many people to become "somebody." Now it's Gloria's turn. It is a pity, like Gloria exclaims, when a person has to "bury the thing that you love the most" because she lacks basic support.

NOTES

1. H. Trask, *From a Native Daughter: Colonialism and Sovereignty in Hawai'i* (Monroe, Maine.: Common Courage Press, 1993), 156-57.

2. Please keep in mind that some of the words and phrases that Gloria uses are in Hawai'i Creole English, commonly called Pidgin. It is considered a language of local island culture.

3. J. Chinen, *Hawai'i Community for the Humanities into the Marketplace: Working-class Women in the Twentieth Century Hawai'i* (Honolulu: Hawai'i Committee for the Humanities, 1988); J. Chinen, "Women in the Labor Force in America and in Hawai'i," in *Working in America and in Hawai'i—A Humanities Guide* (Honolulu: Hawai'i Committee for the Humanities, 1988); H. Trask, "Aloha Industry, for Hawaiian Women, Tourism Is Not a Neutral Industry," *Cultural Survival Quarterly* 16 (1992): 50-60; H. Trask, *From a Native Daughter.*

4. See J. Horsman, *Something in My Mind besides the Everyday: Women and Literacy* (Toronto, Canada: Women's Press, 1990); W. Luttrell, *Schoolsmart and Motherwise: Working-class Women's Identity and Schooling* (New York: Routledge, 1997). K. Rockhill, "Literacy as Threat/Desire: Longing to Be Somebody," *TESL-Talk* 20 (1) (1990): 89-110.

5. G. Spangenberg, *Even Anchors Need Lifelines: Public Libraries in Adult Literacy* (New York: Spangenberg Learning Resources and the Center for the Book, 1996).

▪ 2 ▪

"I Know This Is the Place for Me"

Stories of Library Literacy Learners and Programs

JOHN COMINGS, SONDRA CUBAN, HANS BOS, and CATE TAYLOR

I know education is the way out. It is the way out of poverty. That is what is keeping me from getting out of poverty. No education. So I made up my mind. I said, Ok. Second Start. It has done a lot for me.

Sometimes you get upset. You think, why me? I am not supposed to be at Second Start. That is how I feel. My thoughts tell me I am not supposed to be here. But when it comes out on paper, I know this is the place for me. I told someone, "If I can only get what I think inside my head out on this paper." You feel trapped. You wonder, "When am I ever going to stop coming here?" I have been coming here for two years. Two years. I am able to write essays now but still it is not good enough. I want to be able to write a book. I want to be able to take a regular college course, without being afraid.

So it is not good enough. People tell me I am too hard on myself. And maybe that is why I do not go farther. Wanting so much for myself. And fear. It is hard to deal with. But I know you have to keep trying if you want something. I know that. I think that is my main problem. Wanting to give up. Getting angry with the whole process. Learning is such a long process. You really have to have patience. It is a long process. You have to keep trying, I know that.[1]

Selected sections of this chapter were drawn from "So I Made Up My Mind: Introducing a Study of Adult Learner Persistence in Library Literacy Programs" by John Comings and Sondra Cuban, published by MDRC and DWRD (Dewitt Wallace-Reader's Digest Fund) and LWRD (Lila Wallace-Reader's Digest Fund), 2000.

Resonja Willoughby and other learners in library literacy programs share their worlds with us in many ways. Student writings, which are available in most library literacy programs today, are one way to learn about library literacy learners and their worlds. In these stories, students reveal their struggles, progress, and dreams, and share impressions of their lives with us. By reading learners' stories and listening to them read their own words back to themselves, we can learn why they have come to literacy programs, how they engage with these programs, what their worlds outside of these programs are like, and why they persist in their efforts to learn.

Student writings also can inform us about what works and what does not in library literacy programs from the perspective of learners. This genre has been fostered by Lucy Jane Bledsoe in her recent book called *Working Parts* (1997), in which her main character, upon entering a library literacy program, moves from feeling like an alien to a "new reader" who is a part of the world of the public library:

> I pushed open the library door, walked in like I knew what I was doing, then panicked. All those books made me short of breath, a little dizzy. I leaned against the copy machine and willed myself not to turn around and walk out again.[2]

The main character echoes Resonja's feelings of doubt, "my thoughts tell me I'm not supposed to be here." What can programs do to lessen these feelings and allow for greater student participation?

We have initiated a study of library literacy programs focusing specifically on the problems of learner participation and persistence in these programs. This study is funded by the Lila Wallace-Reader's Digest Fund through its Literacy in Libraries Across America (LILAA) Initiative, and by the U.S. Department of Education's Office of Educational Research and Improvement. We have begun collecting student writings; interviewing students, staff, and other literacy providers; and gathering socio-demographic and participation data on all students in five library literacy programs participating in the LILAA initiative. In addition to collecting information from students, we are conducting extensive observations of these programs to learn more about how they can help learners like Resonja persist in their education. The findings from this study will assist in improving program practices and making programs more accessible to people with low literacy levels.

The LILAA persistence study will also explore the role that libraries play in adult education. Library literacy programs are part of a national system of adult education that is supported by federal, state, local, and private funds. Many other entities in this system, such as community colleges and school districts, serve more adults and have larger budgets. Libraries, however, bring their own strengths to this system; they are permanent institutions in local communities that have many resources to support adult learning—for instance, accessible facilities, extensive referral systems and collections of books, technology, and access to a large group of potential tutors, including retirees and casual library users. Moreover, unlike other programs and education providers, libraries do not generally receive funding that depends on how quickly they move students into employment or into more advanced programs. Consequently, libraries are uniquely accessible to students with very low initial literacy levels, special learning needs, or for those with needs for flexible scheduling. Many of these students have no other education providers to turn to for help in increasing their literacy.

We are actively working with program directors and staff at five library literacy programs to explore ways in which these programs can better support student persistence. The five libraries participating in the study are:

- New York Public Library in New York City
- Greensboro Public Library in North Carolina
- Redwood City Public Library in California
- Queens Borough Public Library in New York City
- Oakland Public Library in California

The programs were selected for the study because they operate high-quality literacy programs that serve a sizeable number of adult students, and because they are developing new practices designed to help students remain engaged longer, to attract new students, and to better help students pursue their dreams and goals.

The programs in our study provide rich opportunities for students to share their worlds with us—in media ranging from student writings and art projects to interviews. Student-produced learning materials and student-led activities are a showcase for student progress in learning and literacy, and they encourage continued engagement by all the students in a program, transforming it from a simple classroom into a community of learning.

Opportunities abound for learners to share their stories in published formats, in stapled or loosely bound booklets, or on banners or columns for everyone to see. Sometimes these stories are dictated to a tutor, and sometimes they are written and revised by students. Student writings are also housed on the Web or are given voice by actors.

In addition to studying student-produced materials and student activities, we are conducting extensive in-depth interviews with students over a two-year period. These interviews, which follow and incorporate the students' life stories, will enable us to gain a greater understanding of student persistence by following it into people's lives outside the literacy programs, and by recording patterns and unique experiences of persistence from the perspectives of learners. We also will collect program participant data on all students over time, which will allow us to describe patterns of attendance and to relate them to the in-depth stories gathered from students and staff. In order to create a holistic picture of persistence from different perspectives, we are studying persistence with multiple methods, at different points in time, and in a variety of library literacy programs spread throughout the country.

As part of the LILAA initiative since 1996, the selected libraries have made concerted efforts to improve their literacy programs. In August 1999, the Wallace-Reader's Digest Funds renewed their support for the LILAA initiative until 2002 to enable these libraries (1) to implement strategies to improve adult learner persistence, and (2) to participate in this study. The strategies that each library will employ to increase adult learner persistence are still being refined; they include childcare, transportation, new curriculum, expanded hours of operation, teacher and tutor training, new instructional approaches, and changes in the intake process and orientation of new students. The LILAA persistence study will help the participating library literacy programs learn from their experiences and will share those experiences with the field of adult literacy. The study seeks to describe the strategies that the programs develop to foster persistence, the way in which the programs change as a result of implementing these strategies, and the way in which students' persistence changes. Hearing and studying the stories of persistence, as told by students and program staff, will offer researchers a window into learning more about the wider phenomenon of student persistence.

Of the 1,067 public libraries responding to the survey, most (94.1%) provide information about literacy services in their community—or refer potential learners to adult literacy programs. . . . Of significance is that nearly one-third (30.1%) of the libraries responded that they "directly" provide adult literacy services— that is, they "lend professional staff, library materials, and/or financial support to the instructional process." *Survey*, p.17, *Impact of Library Services in Libraries*

How important are libraries' direct contributions to adult literacy? Conservative estimates (derived from survey data) are that libraries together spend $25.9 million dollars annually on literacy programs for adults. They are serving over 43,000 learners in Adult Basic Education, over 31,000 learners in English as a Second Language and nearly 20,000 in Family Literacy. *Survey Executive Summary*

Stories of the Five Literacy Programs

The New York Public Library

The New York Public Library (NYPL) is known worldwide for its extensive research collections, which serve scholars in every academic discipline, and for its branch library system. Since the nineteenth century, the Seward branch on the Lower East Side and the Aguilar branch in Spanish Harlem have been two of the most important institutions in the country for helping immigrants assimilate into life in the United States. Today, immigrants still come to the NYPL for English instruction, preparation for citizenship tests, and reading materials in their own languages.

The NYPL is home to Centers for Reading and Writing (CRWs) at 8 of its 85 branches. The CRWs are found in three of New York's five boroughs; Staten Island has one, Manhattan has four, and the Bronx has three. Most CRWs specialize in small-group instruction led by volunteer tutors. Most of the adults who seek out services are African American, Afro-Caribbean, or Latino, and the staff reflects the ethnicity of the students. The LILAA persistence study will focus its research efforts on three CRWs:

- The Wakefield branch, one of the oldest CRWs, is located in a residential neighborhood in the Bronx and serves mostly Afro-Caribbean adults. The CRW resembles a school auditorium. The staff is Afro-Caribbean and uses materials and curricula that reflect students' cultures and interests such as employment, taxation, and health.

- The Fordham branch library is in a dense and energetic business district of the Bronx and houses its busy CRW in several rooms at the back of the library. The CRW expands into other areas of the library in the evenings, when small-group instruction is offered. In one room, computers are arranged like a small computer laboratory, where students can share information as they work on their computers in a lively environment.

- The Seward branch is located in Manhattan, on the Lower East Side. To reach the program, students climb steep stairways to a bright room filled with plants. At the entrance to the CRW is a column labeled "Milestones" that displays students' accomplishments. Lining this large space is a well-read multicultural book collection. The program serves diverse students, who gather in small groups around tables.

Among the strongest aspects of the NYPL program are its adult literacy collection and its ability to capture student voices in writings that the program publishes. Many of these writings focus on the role of learning in students' families and cultures. Each year, students participate in the citywide All Write program, at which professional actors read students' writings in public as part of a student recognition ceremony.

(See also Decklan Fox, chapter 10.)

Greensboro Public Library

Greensboro Public Library (GPL) is the fourth-largest library system in North Carolina. Ten years ago, the library led a community effort to address the needs of adults who have low literacy. This initiative grew into the Community of Readers, which has since developed a plan called Literacy 2000. The GPL supports adult education at two of its nine branches: Chavis and Glenwood.

- The Chavis branch calls itself the Lifelong Learning branch because of its extensive adult literacy collection and computer lab, and because it works with all segments of the population, from children to adults. Every week two teachers from the local community college teach afternoon and evening GED and adult literacy classes. The computer lab provides adults and children with instruction and access to word-processing software and e-mail. A welfare-to-work program provides participants with basic skills in conjunction with critical thinking and leadership skills.

- The Glenwood branch is in a working-class neighborhood that has attracted many refugees and immigrants from all over the world. The library is housed in an attractive modern building that is a source of pride to the community. It offers a myriad of services including one-on-one and small-group English-language instruction, family literacy classes, a computer lab, and a collection of multicultural reading materials. On a typical day, students are involved in various activities throughout the library; students might go from reading a newspaper with their tutor to working on Rosetta Stone, a computerized learning program, in the computer lab. A family literacy program funded by the local Junior League also operates in the children's room.

The strengths of the GPL literacy program include a whole-community approach, which fosters collaboration among students and staff in a personalized environment. The program's multicultural emphasis supports the participation of the growing immigrant population.

(See also Steve Sumerford, chapter 12.)

Redwood City Public Library, California

Project READ is housed in the Redwood City Public Library, which was once a fire station. The program's geographical area is home to more than 15,000 adults who do not have a high school diploma or a GED, as well as to the affluent, well-educated employees of high-tech companies around Redwood City. Project READ emphasizes student-centered curriculum and instruction. The one-on-one tutoring fills a gap left by the school district and community college programs, which only offer traditional classroom instruction.

At four local schools, the library supports the Kids in Partnership Program, which helps at-risk teens and children improve their reading, writing, and English skills. The teens tutor the children, which improves the skills of both. In the evening, small groups of parents are tutored while their children play learning games and receive homework assistance. This intergenerational approach helps build self-esteem and provides children with positive models of reading.

The strengths of Project READ include its holistic approach, which treats students and their families as active participants in the process of instruction. The staff, students, and tutors communicate regularly about instruction and how to improve it, discussing what works and what does not. This process has both yielded an innovative training program for tutors on how to teach adults with learning disabilities and an emphasis on providing literacy services to the whole family.

(See also Kathy Endaya, chapter 8.)

Queens Borough Public Library, New York City

The Queens Borough Public Library (QBPL) is one of the nation's oldest and largest library systems, and serves one of the most ethnically diverse populations in the country. Immigrants from 100 countries—who speak more than 50 languages—use the system, which comprises the central library and 62 branches. Six branches house adult learning centers (ALCs). A manager who has a professional background in adult literacy leads each of the six ALCs. Three of the ALC's six branches are part of the LILAA persistence study:

- The Flushing branch, the library's busiest, is located in a commercial district densely populated by immigrants from all over the world. The ALC is located near the library entrance, on the lower level, and houses its literacy program showcasing a computer lab, a large self-study area, and a glass-encased room where literacy learners can receive tutoring.

- The Central branch serves adult students in bustling Jamaica, Queens, across from the main library. This small, carpeted center has one room in the back for conversation classes, a computer lab, and a large classroom where pre-GED classes are offered. Shelves are filled with self-study materials. Small-group instruction takes place around tables spread throughout the ALC.

- The Rochdale Village branch houses a smaller program that serves Adult Basic Education (ABE) students in a predominantly African-American neighborhood. This ALC occupies a small area inside the library and provides literacy tutoring for multilevel students in diverse subject areas by tutors, some of whom are teachers. It also houses an extensive, well-used book collection.

Among the ALC's strengths as an adult literacy program are centers' literacy collections that can be checked out by adult students. The library recently published new tutor-training manuals, the Queens Kaleidoscope series, each of which focuses on a specific theme, such as using library resources more effectively. It also publishes *The Open Door,* a journal of student writing. Additionally, a student newsletter and a tutor newsletter developed by students and staff are available. The ALCs are open and accessible for as many hours each day as possible, and they have recently focused on improving reading instruction.

(See also Bruce Carmel and Anita Citron, chapter 11.)

Oakland Public Library, California

Second Start is part of the Oakland Public Library. Almost 50 percent of Oakland's population is African American, as are 85 percent of Second Start's students. The program offers African-American thematic literary events, and the program's large multicultural collection is filled with books that reflect African-American culture and the community surrounding Second Start.

Founded in 1984, Oakland's Second Start program has a multiethnic staff. Many of the program's students are not served by other adult education services in the area because they have far lower literacy skills than those programs are prepared to handle. At Second Start, these students receive personalized attention.

Second Start offers family literacy activities, one-on-one tutoring, small-group instruction in spelling and math, and pre-GED classes. A large computer center forms the centerpiece of Second Start. In this room, students help one another with their writing, work on the Internet, practice typing, and use educational software.

Second Start does not have a rigid educational agenda or philosophy. Its focus on the empowerment of students is reflected in students' published writings. Widespread recognition has greeted the program's latest publication, *Women of Oakland: A Book of Life Stories Told by Women in the Second Start Adult Literacy Program,* which contains interviews conducted by an adult literacy student.

Second Start provides an energetic environment. Its informal meeting room is a place to share food donated by neighborhood restaurants, and smaller rooms are available for tutoring and for classes in art, yoga, and stress management. Spelling classes are popular. Second Start is fun, encouraging, and responsive, and it offers leadership opportunities for students.

(See also Leslie McGinnis, chapter 3.)

The LILAA study will produce comprehensive stories of students' experiences inside these library literacy programs. This holistic approach to looking at persistence will provide critical insights that will lead to the types of literacy services that are beneficial and rewarding to the main stakeholders, like Resonja.

NOTES

1. Resonja Bell Willoughby, "Education Is the Way Out," in Sandra Hare (ed.), *Oakland Readers* (Oakland, Calif.: Oakland Public Library, 1996).

2. Lucy Jane Bledsoe, *Working Parts: A Novel* (Seattle: Seal Press, 1997), p. 3.

▪ 3 ▪

A Place in the World

Building a Learner-Centered
Participatory Literacy Program

LESLIE McGINNIS

Participatory literacy education is a philosophy as well as a set of practices. It is based on the belief that learners—their characteristics, aspirations, backgrounds, and needs—should be at the center of literacy instruction. This belief implies that the relationship between learners and program staff is collaborative. The traditional literacy education model places skills at the center and implies a hierarchical relationship between educators (who know the skills) and students (who need to learn the skills). Thus, learners in participatory efforts help to define, create, and maintain the program; those in traditional programs are merely asked to receive it. Adult educators in traditional programs sometimes claim that they begin from where the student is. However, even when information is solicited from students, the power in the program is not shared.[1]

Second Start

At Oakland Public Library, in our Second Start Adult Literacy Program, we have spent the last five years changing our literacy program into a learner-centered participatory literacy model, with great success and more than a few lessons learned.

There have been other successful literacy programs based on the participatory literacy model as detailed in the landmark book *Participatory*

Literacy Education.[2] These literacy programs, for the most part, are run by community-based organizations. The challenge of instituting learner-centered participatory literacy education in a library literacy program is that we operate in public libraries, which, despite some instances of enlightened management style, are still often bureaucratic, hierarchical institutions. How to make our rather radical philosophy of participatory literacy education (and thus, if we are to be true to our vision, participatory program management) fit the expectations and demands of our hierarchical organization? And how to take the challenge a step further, and use our experiences in learner-centered education as a model that might instruct our coworkers and supervisors in the library world? These are challenges we are still working on.

Luckily, at Oakland Public Library, as in other public libraries throughout the country, the hierarchical management model has been flattening, and much of the library's business is done by cross-functional, cross-classification teams, rather than by administrators acting in isolation. It is now a given that this more inclusive way of doing business is more effective and efficient, as well as more fun. This has made our challenge of increasing teamwork and staff participation in the management of the literacy program a bit easier. But we have taken the flattening of the bureaucracy one step further by including library users (adult learners) in the decision-making process, another notion that isn't new to libraries. Libraries have always been customer service oriented, and have always set up their programs and collections to meet the needs of their customers, the library patrons. Libraries have been assiduous about doing customer satisfaction surveys and responding to written and spoken requests from the community. Libraries have tended to have grassroots citizen advisors on their commissions and boards.

As a public librarian, I have the stereotypical librarian's love of order. A learner-centered participatory literacy program can go against a librarian's dearest wish for an orderly world. It can be messy. It can be loud. It can throw itself in your face. It can show you that you don't know all you thought you knew, or that you aren't as tolerant of differences as you thought you were. It can be chockful of misspellings and incomplete sentences. Its grammar can make you cringe. But the unexpected breakthroughs, the suggestions that show true genius, the heart and the courage and the imaginative problem solving of adult literacy students, tutors, and staff working together far outweigh the messiness and are truly inspiring.

As director of the literacy program, I also have to confess that sometimes decisions are still made at the top. The real world does still dictate
hierarchy. And sometimes, when time is of the essence, a director's ultimate responsibility for the program's success or failure means he/she must
make the difficult decisions alone and not collaboratively. When the decisions are made "by the boss," I try to take into account staff and student
input and reflect their concerns as much as possible.

Thoughts on the program:

- Participatory
- Everyone's a learner
- Change
- Caring
- Joy or bliss as an end
- What is the definition of literacy?
- No ego
- Teamwork, flattened bureaucracy
- Confidence building
- Self-strengthening
- Share power

Our Vision

Our vision of learner-centered participatory literacy education, as it
evolves, is a continuum where everyone is included in making program
development decisions and devising strategies to improve our literacy services. We are striving for complete participation, though we realize it
is not always possible, and that not everyone (staff, students, tutors)
will respond to and flourish in a participatory learning and work
environment.

We had been working toward this vision for some time. Our first steps
were the creation of our Oakland Readers series, which recognized the

validity, power, and effectiveness of our students' voices as curriculum. But until we looked closely at our program with new eyes, we thought this was learner-centered enough. It wasn't. The staff still decided the direction of the literacy program and the content of the classes. Tutors still used a top-down banking model of teaching. Our reality did not live up to our vision.

It took a three-year grant from the Lila Wallace-Reader's Digest Fund to encourage and enable us to begin setting up a truly learner-centered literacy program. Some highlights of changes we made include: we hired students to be on our staff, set up advisory groups of students, changed our way of doing business in the literacy office, changed our mission statement, and changed our public relations materials. We also changed our intake and assessment procedures to make them more learner-centered. Our initial intake session went from a 45-minute experience to an hour and a half, and became a dialogue rather than a "test" administered top-down. As one staff person said, "On an individual basis, we ask learners what their goals are and teach to those goals. This is contrary to regular school, where even bright children are controlled by their teachers."

Our classes and small groups now reflect the participatory approach. The curriculum will not work unless learners participate. Classes are joyous; facilitators continually check with learners. "Is this working for you?" is asked all the time. The participatory, learner-centered model actually makes it easier to teach multilevel groups. The learners' participation guides the teacher to the curriculum and in some cases actually creates the day's lesson on the spot.

> Foremost, it is important to recognize that nonreading adults are the creators of their own social lives, as imperfect as those lives may appear by middle-class standards. They participate in the ongoing creation and maintenance of the social world in which they live. Their inherent dignity is at the heart of the belief that they are not only able but that it is their right to participate in creating programs that are supposed to serve their interests.[3]

Suggestions about curriculum come from staff and learner input and experience. There is a lot we don't know or hear about, though. We need to be inclusive to make curriculum work, because adults want a curriculum that is relevant to their lives. Participatory education works better than the old "banking model" for all areas: program development, program management, curriculum development, instructional strategies, and tutor training.

When discussing our vision of participatory education, we see our program providing open-ended education with no timelines, deadlines, or pressures. We want our program to be reliable, a permanent fixture in our students lives, a safe place, a place to chill, a place they can come back to when they are ready to try again. We, as a staff, see ourselves "reinforcing the dignity of the African American who has been permanently humiliated," as one Second Start staff member said, and other people whose lack of education has made them victims and targets of abuse. We want to provide unconditional love to our learners, and continually question our own assumptions about people and how they learn. Patrick takes his hat off. That is progress. Kaddy signs up for all the classes, despite objections from her over-protective husband. We all rejoice.

Our Work Lives Change

In instituting our vision, we saw our work lives change. Staff had to become even more responsive to individual students and to their crises. Our workdays became unpredictable because our learners' lives are unpredictable. We have more work because we are responsive; we created more work for ourselves by listening and responding.

Assessing the effectiveness of our literacy program in the first five years of learner-centered business is a little more complicated than assessing learner skills.

How do we know we're being effective? We see learner progress on monthly reports, checkups, milestone charts, and in class participation. We see notes that parents have received from their children's teachers, saying their children are now reading at grade level thanks to Families for Literacy participation. We see positive changes in students' skills and abilities and self-esteem, and in their progress toward meeting personal goals. How do we know we're being effective? We know it. We live it. We see the signs of success around us every day because the learners are so involved in the program. Now our challenge is to show other stakeholders and funders in their language, that we're being effective, without using standard instruments or tests, but by painting a picture of a learner-centered learning community.

We know we're being effective with our participatory learning model when learners:

- Show joy
- Have good attendance
- Stay with the program
- Trust us
- Succeed in jobs and school
- Go beyond basic skills
- Bring families, children, neighbors, and friends to the program
- Donate time and effort and goods to the literacy program
- Achieve personal goals

When tutors:

- Set up a safe and open lesson time with their students
- Become good listeners
- Encourage learners to communicate their dreams
- Understand how to break those dreams down into lessons and curricula
- Show insight and cross-cultural, cross-class understanding
- Rejoice in diversity
- Are learners themselves

Let go of notions of what "they want to teach" and replace them with "what the learner wants to learn."

SUGGESTIONS FOR BECOMING LEARNER-CENTERED AND PARTICIPATORY

1. Form learner advisory groups; host student assemblies and informal meetings with learners to get input on program changes and curricula. Our student assemblies led to the creation of our popular spelling and art classes, plus a drastic revision in the content of our Families for Literacy Program.
2. Hire learners when possible and involve them in program development.
3. Build instruction around learner goals. Be specific in delineating goals, even the smallest goals, so that tutors and teachers and students will have learner-centered direction (example 1).
4. Create learner-centered curriculum processes and, when possible, learner-centered curriculum books and other materials (example 2).
5. Always involve students/learners in decision making. Be creative in meeting needs (e.g., yoga class, stress class).
6. Craft assessment procedures and forms so that there is some student self-assessment.
7. Create and take advantage of student leadership opportunities. Involve students in conferences and meetings whenever possible.

The Check-in

An easy way to get your literacy classes, tutoring sessions, staff meetings, and learner advisory group meetings to become learner-centered and participatory in a hurry is to institute the "check-in" at the beginning of every meeting.

What is a check-in? It's a chance for the participants to tell the group how they are feeling, and for the group to support and understand all of its members. For example, in staff meetings, we go around the table with each staff person checking in. Some days it is simple, "I feel good today," or "I'm happy because my child is getting good grades." Other days it is more complicated, as people do feel that they have to unburden themselves sometimes, or explain themselves. This happened one day when a staff member talked about feeling depressed because she didn't know much about her ancestors, that the background of slavery had made her parents "be quiet about my roots." This check-in statement became the basis for a staff discussion on the spot, making the staff member who brought up the issue feel supported and listened to, and also making other staff members see other areas of common experience. Eventually this staff person, who was also a learner, took a life-transforming trip to Africa and regained pride in her ancestry. The check-in at literacy classes and tutoring sessions produces ideas and topics for curriculum building and language experience, but it also clears the student's head of problems that might have stood in the way of their being fully attentive and ready to learn that day.

The check-in is also a good strategy for making people, especially learners, feel as if they're in a caring, supportive environment. This keeps learners coming back to the program, even on days when their personal problems seem overwhelming. If the literacy program is seen as a place where people care, where a certain amount of time is spent each lesson on the learner's "problem story," and when that story becomes the basis for a literacy lesson and is resolved with the help of other learners, then students are more likely to return to the program, for literacy and for assistance with daily obstacles.

In a class situation, and even with a tutor, the check-in is a chance for the students to hear their own voices in a new context. This is especially important for those learners who are shy and hesitant about talking in a group or about speaking to their tutor. The check-in will encourage students to participate more. And when this technique is used regularly it becomes part of the culture of the literacy program.

Check-in Problem Story Elements, an Example

During check-in, a learner explained why she had missed a few of the past meetings and why she was so late on that day. She had had to go to her child's school to see the principal and the teacher due to the child's disruptive behavior in class. The teacher was upset; the principal was threatening to suspend the child; the child was surly and noncompliant and she, the student, told the class "she was at the end of her rope."

Allowing the learners to take the lead, the literacy teacher deliberately kept quiet, while clustering learner comments on the board. He listened to the learners, but he also listened for the appropriate moments to interject a quiet, nonauthoritative comment and a story element in an analytical way in the ongoing discussion. Learners were already analyzing and interpreting the implications of the check-in story, the meaning of the *plot* and the *conflicts* in the story, but they were not using those terms.

An opportunity came when someone raised the issue of the teacher's attitude and behavior toward the child. The teacher asked about the setting in the room. How large was the classroom and how many kids were in it? What was the atmosphere in the room? What was the teacher's tone of voice? Did it change when the child's parent (the literacy student) came in? What time of day was it? The learner began to answer some of these questions, and some of the other learners ran with the ball. Again, without prompting, someone raised a point about the teacher's *point of view.*

What the teacher began to see happening, very gradually and not always precisely, was an initial, haphazard use of story elements. At first they were just descriptors that learners had picked up from the teacher. Only gradually were they used as tools in analyzing, interpreting, and helping others and themselves to resolve their problem-stories that were revealed and shared as check-ins.

Some learners were able to complete or resolve their stories. Indeed, the learner's problem story that was used as an example was satisfactorily managed if not resolved. It turned out that one of the reasons, predictably, that the child was disruptive in school, was that one of the child's relatives was a substance abuser and was disrupting the child's household. The learner had not seen the connection, at first, between what was happening to the child at home and his behavior in school.

Difficulties with the Learner Participation Model

Our biggest difficulty has been the lack of time and resources to not only involve all of our learners but to carry through on their suggestions. This is something we will work on for a lifetime. Also, many learners are not used to being asked for input, don't have the background or the time to think, and thus don't have much to tell us at first.

CHECKLIST FOR LEARNER INVOLVEMENT

1. Learner advisory group (standing group)
2. Learner advisory groups (ad hoc)
3. Learners planning special events and celebrations
4. Learner assemblies annually or semiannually
5. Telephone surveys
6. Always consult learners.
7. Rethink strategies to include learners, so that each day a learner is involved.
8. Learners evaluating curriculum, program, tutors, teachers
9. Unearth special talents of learners; capitalize on these talents with art shows, baking contests, and by creating an environment where learners can shine and participate.
10. Host special informal learning opportunities, such as field trips to museums, and use the trip as a chance to solicit learner input.

The Civil Service System has made it difficult to hire literacy students in our program. It took much searching and many false starts to finally find a job classification (Student Trainee) that doesn't require a high school diploma or GED.

Some tutors and staff do not agree with our new vision and philosophy and have actively resisted the participatory model, feeling much more familiar with the old model, which is how most of us experienced education. Gradually, those who were uncomfortable either adjusted (after seeing the benefits of learner-centered instruction) or left to find work in a more traditional literacy setting.

The Director's Role, Qualities, and Dilemma

The literacy director must learn to be an "allowing" administrator, one who is big enough to give in, look foolish, be wrong, hear criticism, go in a different direction, learn from staff and learners. Some of the dilemmas

ADMINISTRATIVE CHANGES

In order to be true to our vision of a learner-centered participatory literacy program, we had to make the following changes in the administration of our program.

1. Weekly staff meetings are now facilitated on a rotating basis, with each staff member, including learners, being responsible for collecting agenda items and running the meeting. We also instituted the "check-in" at the beginning of each staff meeting, in order to give each person a chance to participate.

2. Teamwork and collaborative decision making now characterize the way we do business at Second Start. Projects are assigned to teams, meetings are held with flip charts, brainstorming with the group is the order of the day, and decisions are made in the teams collaboratively, then brought to the staff meeting for final discussion or to the director for final approval. We have 14 staff members, only three of whom are full-time, and this gives us the people with which to create the teams.

3. Curriculum development is now based on the input of learners. We hold student assemblies and canvass students as to curriculum needs and interests. From this we develop new classes and materials, including two new curriculum guides developed from the art class that the learners requested.

4. A print-rich environment has been created in the literacy center, using creations and comments of learners and displaying their achievements prominently. We have pictures and essays on the wall, accomplishments written in learner writing on the milestone chart, and pictures of the families in the family literacy program in two display cases. This shows the learners that the center and the program are theirs.

5. Tutor training was drastically revised to make it more participatory and to model learner-centered participatory literacy instruction for the volunteer tutors.

6. Our brochures and public relations materials were revised to reflect the change in philosophy and to use phrases such as "at Second Start, everyone is a learner."

of a literacy director attempting to institute or "allow" a learner-centered literacy program include:

1. How to pick the learners to hire, involve, encourage. Why not involve all learners?
2. How to allow for maximum growth of staff and learner expertise.
3. So what if the paperwork is not as perfect as it should be?

In a participatory system, personnel selection becomes paramount. This type of setup requires people who can take a lot of individual responsibility, who are flexible, risk-taking, creative people who like to be both part of a team and autonomous. This has meant revising interview questions to reflect new qualities in personnel.

The participatory model requires a lot more coordination and communication. Things happen quickly, unexpectedly, and spontaneously since we want to be able to respond to the learners when they need us and when they are ready to give input or tell us about certain needs.

Sometimes there is so much going on that it is difficult to pull staff away and have the discussion that needs to take place. Staff meetings, which should be sacred, are sometimes sacrificed to other meetings, site visits, or special events.

There are also workload issues that have surfaced. We asked the students to participate, we asked for ideas, we instituted new ideas in addition to keeping some of the old program modes, without adding new staff or other resources. Being open to new ideas and making program changes can result in more work for staff, so that each change must be carefully considered in light of staff time and energy.

Closing Thoughts from a Second Start Learner

Second Start has changed my life. To a certain degree, I'm not ashamed of my reading anymore. I used to be very ashamed. Second Start gave me self-esteem. Most of all, I like the feeling here. I come in here and I don't feel like I'm going to be let down. Nobody's looking down on me. Everyone here have a smile on their face. Everyone's willing to work with you. Nobody never question where you at. They just try to help you go on further than where you are.

CHALLENGES OF CREATING
A LEARNER-CENTERED, PARTICIPATORY
LITERACY PROGRAM

1. The hierarchy and demands of the parent institution (public library) and the public employee labor union may contradict and sometimes undermine the participatory model, confusing staff and learners and, in some cases, preventing implementation of some participatory strategies.

2. Grant deadlines and reporting requirements don't allow enough time for the participatory process of information gathering.

3. The reality of diminished resources will limit the follow-through in learner-centered instruction. The fact that learners and staff give input and ideas that are above and beyond what a program can realistically do may dampen staff and learner interest in participation.

4. Some staff and learners (and tutors) take time to warm up to the idea of participating. Some are not ready, not confident enough, or just plain not interested in this approach.

5. In terms of accountability, state, federal, and other professional standards and measures of program success (including requirements for funding) fit hierarchical programs better than participatory ones.

6. The reality of involving many people in decision making is that it's time-consuming. With so much communication taking place, when does the literacy instruction occur?

I already feel bad because of where I am anyway. Then sometimes, you can tell people make you feel uncomfortable by knowing where you at. People like looking down on people. Here at Second Start it is not like that. People, they accept you. Nobody is focusing on the mistakes you made.

I see that lady at the front desk at Second Start. She started out like me. Now she's working here. There's a place in the world for you.[4]

REWARDS OF CREATING A LEARNER-CENTERED, PARTICIPATORY LITERACY PROGRAM

1. A livelier, more committed and involved staff, tutors, and learners.

2. The literacy program is better able to meet the needs of the learners because they know the learners better and have heard firsthand what the learners need and want from a literacy program.

3. The curriculum is more meaningful and engaging; learners participate more in learning, thus learn more, and are more persistent in their quest for education.

4. The literacy program operates with a wealth of diverse and excellent ideas.

5. Better, more productive staff meetings.

6. More trust among staff, learners and tutors; a feeling of support, and family.

7. People work harder, better, and easier.

8. Tutor training is more effective; tutors are more thoughtful and encourage learner participation.

9. Staff models good communication.

10. Work done in teams strengthens the bonds between team members and strengthens the whole staff.

11. Staff, learners, and tutors are modeling strategies for community involvement.

NOTES

1. *Participatory Literacy Education,* ed. Arlene Fingeret and Paul Jurmo (San Francisco: Jossey-Bass, 1989), p. 5.

2. *Participatory Literacy Education.*

3. Ibid., p. 9.

4. Levester Pierson, "There's a Place in the World for You," *Oakland Readers,* 4th series (Oakland, Calif.: Second Start Adult Literacy Program, 1996).

.4.

Relearning Literacy and Leadership in a Library-Based Literacy Program

SHERRY DROBNER

We used to see education as privilege for few people
But now we give education to all.
We used to sacrifice family for work
But now we value family more then anything.
We used to take relationships for granted
But now we strive for better.
We are educated.
We are one family.
We are validated.
We used to be as cold as strangers
But now we feel warm and open-minded.
We used to have pollution everywhere
But now we have balanced ecology.
We used to have family struggles here and there
But now we are supportive.
We are knowledgeable
We are in control.
We are hopeful.[1]

Our program, like many others in California libraries, found its first breath in the one-to-one tutoring model to teach reading. Over the years, we made the transition from individual to small-group tutoring in order to counter the isolation experienced by many of the learners. Inspired by the work of other people around the country, we grew familiar with the programs rooted in the idea of popular education.[2] My meetings and conversations with Michael James, Patricia Medina, Claudia Rivera, and Raul Anorve expanded the possibilities of our work at Alameda County Library. These educators created programs that effectively connected community concerns to the acquisition of literacy skills. The students in these community-based programs used literacy as a tool rather than an end in itself to collectively address the problems in their community. These programs served as models for adult learner leadership and opened the door for our own work on literacy and leadership.

The Notion of Leadership

As a child, leaders in my mind were presidents, conquering military chiefs, and wealthy industrialists who reshaped the landscape of America. These images, primarily created through a school curriculum and the popular media, ignored the heroic deeds of ordinary men and women. Textbooks define historical movements through individual accomplishments. For example: the civil rights movement is often ascribed to Martin Luther King Jr., with a mention of Rosa Parks; the struggles of the farm workers are attributed to César Chávez; and the women's suffragist movement is credited to Susan B. Anthony and a few others.

   We do not know, nor do people usually write about, the countless people who contributed to all these movements. However, people who join movements are leaders as well as followers. They think, they listen, they exchange ideas, and they act upon ideas. They are part of history and, as part of history, they make history.

Beginning the Leadership Project

The idea of collective leadership and civic responsibility guided the project of the Alameda County Library from 1996 to 1999. As our project unfolded, we witnessed clear examples of how the great capacity for leadership rested not in the few, but in the many. Our program, "Students Be Tutors," is intended to deepen the participation and leadership capacity of the students through an intensive three-year training and mentorship program.

The participants in the leadership program have names and I am fortunate to know them. They call themselves Joy Tsou, Jack Hwa, Teresa Gonzalez, Darlene Garcia, and Cathy Lewis. Michael James, a key member of the project, describes them as "mainstream Americans, some newly immigrated."[3]

According to Michael, "the students engaged in the project so they would better understand the theory and practice of the approach itself, as well as generate their own ability to teach, get more involved with local issues, and heighten their literacy abilities that they might engage in the discourse of critical pedagogy." Michael continues, "They perceived a need for mainstream community adults such as themselves to develop social consciousness, involve themselves with cultural and political activity, and work to make positive social change."

Leadership through Dialogue

Students met bimonthly with facilitator Michael James to engage in dialogue, examine their basic assumptions about education, and address their broader concerns of moral and social responsibility. The course outline included:

- History and Theory of Education
- Roots of Education for Critical Consciousness
- Dynamics of Facilitation
- Developing Our Own Pedagogy
- Dynamic and Relevant Teaching Activities

Michael says of his classes, "Reading theory was the most challenging activity of the course, whether from the texts of Joan Wink or Paulo Freire or from journal articles on the economy, or descriptions and instructions of teaching activities. We employed a critical approach: reading the text, putting the text into context through interpretive and critical discussion, and then rereading the text."

One student echoes this sentiment. He writes in one of his journals, "The content of the class is not to teach us how to teach but more it teaches us how to think critically, raise questions, analyzing them, relating them to our past experiences, and, finally, connect ourselves to the world. By reading, writing, discussing, role-playing and (really trying out) experimenting, we learn that every one of us is similar, we are on the same boat. We grow together with each other's help and encouragement. We help each other out to bring about our potential."

Finding Themes in Our Work

In addition to the social theory class, students attended two training institutes and weekly classes to learn about Thematic Based Instruction. The Institutes, facilitated by Patsy Medina, offered students a foundation for understanding different approaches to teaching and developing curriculum.[4] Specifically, students focused on the ideas of "generative word" or "generative phrase," whereby the deepest or most important ideas generated by the student become the core curriculum. The theme of the class emerges through student discussion and the teacher is responsible for listening, validating, and using the theme as a basis for class activities. Examples of themes that later emerged in our classes are language and power, discrimination, bilingualism, and cultural assimilation.

When meeting weekly, student and staff reassessed their ideas about literacy. We further explored the use of generative word, and examined the tension we seemed to face when we talked about teaching skills within a meaningful context. Students raised important questions, such as: How do we set aside workbooks to teach grammar? How do we teach phonics and generate meaningful discussion? How do we find out about what issues motivate or stir our students? And, what literacy practices will help our students address these issues?

Through our discussions we decided that thematic instruction required a rethinking of literacy as an individual problem with individual solutions. Our conversations created new directions as we discussed how to build community into our classroom. As a program we wanted to address community needs; however, many of our students came to our classes to seek individual remedies. Embedded within the historical framework of the California Literacy Campaign, the face of adult literacy resembled a learner-centered, one-to-one tutoring program for the achievement of individual goals. Our staff and students in the training program constantly faced the tensions of pursuing literacy work aimed at improving our community through a collective effort, and the reality that students were basically clients seeking services. This contradiction guided our work and fueled the students as they deepened their participation in the project.

The Examination of Literacy, Language, and Culture

By year two of the project, students were ready to deepen their understanding for teaching pedagogy.[5] To embark on this discussion we started once again with a reexamination of our basic assumptions. Students grappled with the question: What is literacy? Is literacy simply decoding words, and writing memos and letters, or do broader purposes exist?

We explicitly examined language and pursued the idea of "critical literacy." Inspired by the work of Brazilian educator Paolo Freire (1970), we examined the liberating aspects of literacy as well as the oppressive possibilities. We started to see how literacy might be used as a sorting tool in educational systems and workplaces, but we recognized how we might gain access to certain domains in our life with improved literacy. We learned how some writers want to keep some readers out of a conversation by the nature of their words and the style of their writing, while other writers make the literacy event more accessible. By understanding how language works, how relationships shape language, how context and relationships alter the power of language, and how language is used as a tool for power, students reconstructed a new way to teach literacy skills.[6]

Darlene says of the class, "When I began reading Joan Wink's book, *Critical Pedagogy: Notes from the Real World,* it helped me reflect on my own education and my life. Wink talks about how people are "put out" by how they look or their economic class. Others labeled me as lower class when I was younger. I was considered poor and didn't have an educational background. I was never engaged in any dialogue in any life situation. After reading *Critical Pedagogy,* I saw how important it is to ask questions. One question I ask myself is Why are things the way they are? I have the right to ask Why am I being 'kept out?' Before I was passive, now I am active through questioning myself and others."

Other students echoed Darlene's preoccupation with questions. Their process of inquiry mushroomed and produced more questions. For example, Michael writes of other questions raised within his course:

- How do you know what you know?
- What are our personal and collective beliefs about history, society, and political reality?
- What keeps adult students from looking at the world in a critical way?
- How can we teach adult students like ourselves to think critically?

All these questions served us well as guides for deep and stimulating conversation. The whole idea of questioning took over our discussions at one point. What are the kinds of questions that need to be asked? How do we know what questions to ask? As students appropriated the role of teacher, we began to reconsider how we framed questions. We distinguished not only between open- and closed-ended questions, but we grew comfortable with the art of asking why—to ourselves and to each other. Ultimately, our questioning about education and literacy dead-ended to broader issues about relationships of power and authority.

Authority and Power in the Classroom

"When I first started this class I worried that too much would be expected from me. Now I know that it is never solely up to the teacher to make the class work. I know that the feedback from students is critical to my learning. Reflection is a difficult act. The teacher/student relationship creates a tension that needs to be explored at all cost. It is in these tensions that learning occurs."

This journal entry, written early on in the project, clearly reveals a specific notion about the role of the teacher. Traditionally, teachers are vested with authority and responsibility. Leaders tend to be vested with similar powers. The classic teacher/leader hero in our cultural stories stands alone and above the crowd. The classic heroic teacher of film emits a boot-camp authoritative air, single-handedly transforming the staff and students. A teacher's authority emerges from the structure of school and the cultural notions attached to "knowledge." Schools are depositories of "knowledge" and teachers are the people who make the "deposits."

In a traditional classroom, the teacher is the leader of a class. The teacher typically decides upon curriculum, generates the instructions, and plans the coursework. Students are expected to follow the teacher's lead.

Our literacy program wanted to examine and reshape this model of learning. We did. We reexamined the paradigm of teacher/student, and in its place created a model by which students were teachers and teachers were learners. As a team, we engaged in a relearning of literacy education.

Although we worked collectively and respectfully, literacy students continued to grant authority to myself and other staff members as teachers. Clearly, in any classroom, certain structures maintain the teacher authority.[7] However, students began early on to understand their own authority vested in them through their life.

Joy tells us, "I had been working with the program for the last five years. We got deeply into a series of practices and theories such as Paulo Freire and critical pedagogy. Now, when I sit back and think about myself, and the changes I made, I realize that I was wrong before. From the study that I have gone through and all the years' experience and practices before me, I found out that the background and education of a student are not that important.

"People are very complex subjects. No matter how much education or what kind of background they had before, they all have some sort of common sense, perception, intelligence, instinct, consciousness, experience, intuition, awareness, wisdom, opinions, logic, or even imagination. Everybody has the ability to create and this ability is based upon all of the above factors. It is not limited only to the highly educated people as what I always thought, but it is true for everybody."

Darlene writes about her own authority stating, "I am learning a lot about myself and about who I am and how important it is to be connected to other people and places. It makes me think about how I can make changes in my life. How questioning is learning and relearning and we are always doing it. Through this class I am more aware. My mind is more open. As an adult I am learning change can be good and allows me to feel powerful."

As a Result of Our Relearning

Although I write a story with a beginning and an end, the process was by no means linear. To prepare students for teaching, it was decided that staff would teach classes and students would pair up with staff and work as co-teachers. At the start of this process students expressed concerns, but as the classes progressed, the team members learned to do "community corrections," work with poetry to teach tense shifts and comprehension, facilitate group learning, and assist with editing. Although the students were acquiring skills to teach the basics of literacy, team members were still fearful about their capacity as tutors.

As the students compared traditional literacy practices and notions with the thinking of Freire and others, they expanded their attention to other elements of the literacy program. Through discussion, role-play, and analysis, students decided that we needed a new student orientation to address the potential conflicts between program goals and student expectations. They restructured the student orientation and launched a video project to offer prospective students an overview of our program philosophy. Michael posed questions, allowing students the freedom to roam with ideas, and encouraging self-reflection. Students explored their ideas about their own roles within the community.

As students grew more comfortable within their roles as program thinkers and planners, new initiatives surfaced. For example, Jack approached me and suggested we involve more students in the teaching process. "Not literacy," he suggested, "but whatever they have talents to share." As a result, he organized new students into the program to teach yoga, painting, candle-making, and flower-arranging. Another student organized students within her apartment complex and started English as a Second Language classes, while another member applied for and secured a job at the library. Now that the grant is completed, three of the team members are part of the program staff working either as instructors or in a program-planning capacity. Several students continued their education at community college. Although the personal journeys of each student are interesting and positive according to their own standards, their transformation of their own image is critical to the broader concept of leadership.

Jack writes, "I have learned new theories, which I will be applying in my teaching. I literally have grown up in the training. I began to ponder the spiritual questions that before I didn't pay much attention to. I listen more carefully when people are talking. The training offers me a great opportunity to see clearly who I am and what I want by back and forth reflecting and questioning the value on myself."

Cathy echoes these sentiments when she says, "I really feel being in a program like this gives me a better sense of myself, also allowing me to connect with the world around me, allowing me to be there for my children when they need me."

Teachers and academics write about transformative learning in adult education. In most contexts, the transformation is depicted as individual change. Our leadership program, according to participant comments, generated change in thinking and change in action. For myself, I learned that a moment does not make a movement. In other words, our leadership group, our classes, and our process were uniquely appropriate to a specific point in time. We had a sufficient number of students who were interested in change, and we had access to specific staff members to facilitate the process. Our experience cannot necessarily be replicated by us or by others. We cannot offer a recipe or how-to workbook for other programs. We can simply provide an account of a handful of lives that made a commitment to step out of the prescribed boundaries of "adult literacy" and relearn ideas of leadership.

The students/teachers conclude, in a statement read to other library literacy directors and staff, "Leadership is not control but making changes. This leadership does not involve one leader only. We need to be open-minded and informative because it is not one person's decision but a group effort. We are training students to know that everybody can be their own leader. Everybody can contribute their own knowledge and that is how we learn and re-learn to change our own life together."

NOTES

1. Written by Cathy Lewis, Darlene Garcia, Joy Tsou, and Jack Hwa, students in the Lila Wallace-Reader's Digest Project "Students Be Tutors," winter 1998.

2. Popular education is a process by which the marginalized or oppressed members of a community engage in dialogue and the reexamination of assumptions commonly held within their culture. This process, commonly associated with the work of Paulo Freire, challenges traditional relationships between teacher authority and student obedience.

3. Michael James is an adult educator with extensive study and practice in popular education.

4. Medina is an experienced adult educator and teacher trainer, known nationally for her work with thematic-based instruction.

5. Pedagogy addresses the overarching philosophy that guides the classroom. Pedagogy is not necessarily concerned with teaching methodology or teaching activities; however, these later items are closely linked. How a teacher defines learning or a learner is a pedagogical issue. How a teacher designs a course is a methodological issue; however, the first is usually linked to the latter.

6. Joan Wink, *Critical Pedagogy: Notes from the Real World,* 2nd ed. (Reading, Mass.: Addison-Wesley, 1999); Ira Shor, *Critical Teaching for Social Change* (Chicago: University of Chicago Pr., 1992).

7. Shor, *Critical Teaching;* H. Giroux, *Teachers as Intellectuals: Toward a Critical Pedagogy of Learning,* Critical Education series (Bergin and Garvey, 1988).

REFERENCES

Freire, Paulo. "The Adult Literacy Process as Cultural Action for Freedom." *Harvard Educational Review* 30, 2 (May 1970): 205–25.

Giroux, H. *Teachers as Intellectuals: Toward a Critical Pedagogy of Learning.* Critical Education series. Bergin and Garvey, 1988.

Shor, Ira. *Critical Teaching for Social Change.* Chicago: University of Chicago Pr., 1992.

Wink, J. *Critical Pedagogy: Notes from the Real World.* 2nd ed. Reading, Mass.: Addison-Wesley, 1999.

▪ 5 ▪

Charting the Course
for Learner Leadership

TAYLOR WILLINGHAM

The benefits of learner involvement in program development and implementation are numerous. Learners have an advantage over literacy practitioners in communicating with and inspiring their peers because they have a shared experience. In some programs, a fellow learner is often the first person new learners meet when they join the program. These learner-leaders are role models and provide ongoing support and motivation. In the spring of 2000, we conducted a survey of library literacy program managers in California to document the level of learner involvement and the benefits the program receives from learners who are performing duties that are critical to the organization, either as paid staff or as volunteers. According to one program manager, "Our learner adds motivation, excitement, and sensitivity to student needs." Another program manager reflected, "The learner helps staff understand what problems the student might be having from a student point of view."

Despite this rosy picture, program managers have also been frustrated in their attempts to increase learner involvement. In response to our sur-

---

Author's note: There has not been a national consensus on whether adults involved in literacy programs prefer the term "student" or "learner." At a recent meeting of learners representing library literacy programs in California, the preference was split equally between the two terms. I will use the terms interchangeably.

vey, program managers indicated that (1) they have a desire to increase learner involvement (e.g., hiring a learner or starting a learner advisory board), and view this strategy as a means to improving the services of their programs; (2) efforts to engage learners in activities beyond attending their tutoring session have not been successful; and (3) individual learners have been active, but that there is a lack of a formal structure for engaging learners as a group. The desire to increase learner involvement in program development, literacy policy, instructional methodology, and accountability is evident in listserv postings, research reports, the formation of VALUE (a national coalition of adult learners), the priorities of literacy supporters like the Wallace Funds, national organizations such as Literacy Volunteers of America (LVA), and in conversations among practitioners and learners. Volunteer-based programs are effective in offering learner-centered instruction, but have been frustrated in their attempts to promote learner involvement in leadership and decision-making positions. For example, one accreditation standard of LVA requiring that programs have a policy articulating the nature of student-centered instruction is a standard most programs are comfortable meeting. Our research reveals, however, that another optional accreditation standard requiring student involvement in all aspects of the program poses a significant challenge, and meeting this standard is a concern to program managers.

A growing number of library-based programs are responding to this challenge by recruiting and hiring learners for paid staff positions. However, this strategy has not been without its own set of challenges. Attempts to bring learners into a more active role in their program often leads to frustration for both the learners and the program managers. We have combined our perspectives as a former program director and a learner advocate, and have been working to understand and document these barriers as a first step toward possible solutions to the challenge.

At a national literacy conference last year, we informally interviewed learners who are paid literacy program staff or are very active volunteers. These learners valued the opportunity to give back to their program and were passionate about the important contributions they make. However, they also complained about being given menial jobs and cited other duties they felt uniquely qualified to perform. At the same time, they acknowledged a need for professional development in order to be effective in their jobs. We questioned them further to determine what skills they wanted to develop. They requested training in public speaking, fielding questions, how to conduct workshops, how to use technology, planning, time management, proposal writing, business writing, what it means to be a board member, parliamentary procedures, and team building. Most important, they needed training in how to be a leader.

Research Methodology

In June 2000 we convened 21 learners who are also paid staff in library literacy programs for a retreat in San José, California.[1] Funded by the California State Library, it was the first time these learners had the opportunity to gather with their peers. These learner-leaders represented rural programs in the northernmost region of the state, just south of the Oregon border to our urban southern partners just north of the Mexico border.[2] These learner-leaders had experience on staff ranging from three months to eight years. Our goals for this retreat were to:

- provide learners with the opportunity to share their experiences and expertise with each other;
- begin to document (i.e., collect job descriptions and resumes) the duties and skills of the participants;
- collect workshop outlines, flyers, publicity materials, and other printed documents developed by the participants;
- identify their staff development needs.

In order to accomplish these goals, we recorded the duties currently being performed by the participants on flip chart sheets. Each learner then took time to share the various workshops, events, and activities they perform in their organization. On our final day together, the learner-leaders posted color-coded dots marked with their initials on the flip chart sheets to identify (1) the tasks they perform, (2) the tasks they perform well, and (3) the tasks they want/need to perform better but need more training to be effective. We then asked them to complete a survey designed to determine their job status (e.g., full-time with benefits, part-time with benefits, contractual without benefits), the degree of autonomy they have in performing their tasks, their greatest contribution to the program, the one thing they would change about their job, and the reason they have not made this change.

Findings

This retreat led to some surprising as well as predictable findings.

FINDING 1
Learner leaders are performing a wide range of highly demanding tasks

When mapped out on flip chart paper, the list of tasks learner-leaders perform in their programs spanned the entire length of one wall. The tasks (when grouped by general duties) include:

High-level administrative: preparing reports, managing and interpreting data, selecting and purchasing materials

Intake, assessment, and matching: enrolling learners, conducting literacy assessments, preparing learner need reports for staff and tutors, conducting one-on-one and group orientations, matching tutors with learners, preparing student contracts

Clerical: entering data, filing, conducting inventory, office work on the computer, answering phones

Counseling: crisis intervention and referral, helping with employment and job placement, problem solving, conducting home visits, conducting support groups

Communication: publishing newsletters, speaking at tutor training

Event planning: organizing social events, organizing learner conferences

Program development: organizing families for literacy programs, leading storytimes, updating learners about program activities at quarterly meetings

Public relations: organizing speakers bureaus, advocating for literacy in the community, public speaking

Needs assessment: researching community needs, surveying tutors and learners, conducting planning meetings with tutors and learners

Training: tutoring, teaching tutor training, conducting small-group tutoring, managing the computer lab

Volunteer management: managing students who donate time, recruiting learners to speak at tutor training

Contrary to our initial interviews, each of these categories contains tasks that require complex skills. These are not menial jobs, but jobs that require the ability to perform difficult tasks with a high degree of competence. As one learner stated ironically, "We're doing counseling and we don't even have degrees!"

FINDING 2
The road from volunteer to staff is not as smooth as program managers might think

Most of the learner-leaders had a history of volunteerism with their programs before becoming paid staff. In most cases, the transition did not include a dramatic change in duties, it simply meant that those duties came with a paycheck. It seems natural, then, to assume that this is an easy transition for the learners. It clearly was not. We cannot say it any better than was said by one of the learners:

> After taking the job, I felt accountable. Before, when I was a volunteer, I did it because I wanted to and the program was grateful. Each and every day, it was like "wow, this is really cool." I was like a kid in a candy store. I was finding out who I was. I was finding me! I would do something and then look at it and think, "that's pretty cool. That's not half bad. I didn't think I could do that." When it turned to being a paid position, I felt like I had to be perfect, but I was coming into the position with imperfect skills. If I screwed up as a volunteer, it wasn't awful, but I felt like I had to be perfect because I was getting paid. I was afforded every opportunity to learn. There was never any pressure other than put on me by myself. It caused me migraines for about three weeks. I had to talk myself through it. I never even expressed it to my boss until a couple of years later. When I did, she said, she never knew, so I guess it didn't show.

FINDING 3
Learners desire additional training in order to be effective in their jobs and to move into positions of increasing responsibility

These learners had a strong sense that they were not adequately prepared to perform their jobs effectively, much less move into positions of increasing responsibility either within or outside of the field. They further expressed frustration that they were not receiving the kind of training that would support them then and in the future. One learner reflected that the sum total of her transition from volunteer to staff was to be given a key to the front door and her own desk. As one learner articulated, "You have those outgoing learners . . . they go out and get it. I know how to run that program, but if I want to move on? I don't know how to move on." Another learner pleaded, "Can we have some kind of career path to follow? How do you see yourself in the future?"

FINDING 4
Learner-leaders feel as though they have abandoned their own educational goals

This sentiment rang through stronger than any other theme over the course of the weekend and was stated most profoundly when one learner commented, "I need more of the basics to get a GED. I'm not saying that I didn't get anything from the program, but I want to go to the next step, but I'm scared. How can my program help me to succeed so that I can tell learners this program has helped me to succeed for *real?* How can I talk to my students saying 'you can do it' when I need to move to the next level?" This same student went on to say, "I'm still a student. I want to grow inside!"

Another learner echoed, "Do you know that the words I use every day I don't know how to spell? I want to not only do it, but to learn it. I want to claim it."

A sentiment that came out very strongly was the idea that students want to claim their own learning but feel blocked by program managers who are the gatekeepers to the learner-leaders' pursuit of their own literacy goals. Despite this barrier, some of these learner-leaders have developed innovative ways to continue their education. One learner who confided that she recruits incoming tutors for herself stated, "I find myself working and not reading for days at a time. They say I graduated from the program, but there's no way. I check my own tutors out. I walk around and solicit them." Another learner refused additional hours so that he could continue pursuing his learning goals.

One learner's program has demonstrated leadership and a commitment to her literacy achievement by making literacy a part of this learner's annual staff development goals. While this is a start, we clearly have a long way to go before we can respond to the challenge issued by one learner: "Don't split me up. Learners put their own educational goals on the back burner. I shouldn't have to sacrifice my own goals. I want to grow; take me to the next level."

FINDING 5
The learner-leaders feel a tension between being paid staff and being an advocate for learners

This concern revolved around internal relationships (i.e., not knowing how to talk to fellow staff, a sense of lack of internal support). Further exploration revealed that some learner-leaders expected that all of their ideas would be fully embraced by fellow staff because they were, after all, hired to "be the voice" of the learner. When they were treated like "one of the gang" and their ideas were subjected to the same critique as their colleagues, they took it personally and felt as though they were not being taken seriously. It is a human condition to feel rejection when one's ideas are subject to scrutiny. However, one learner, who has been on staff for a number of years, countered with the argument that being on staff makes you a part of the team, which means that you have to work together and be willing to let your ideas be taken apart.

Another learner-leader shared that she felt talked down to when she first accepted her position. She emphatically reminded her coworkers that she, and all other learners, were adults deserving of their respect. Only when she was able to step back and evaluate the dynamic relationships was she able to see that her sense of being "talked down to" was really about a difficult relationship with a colleague and a difference in style.

Without further study, it is difficult to determine the reason for this tension. Perhaps these learner-leaders have become token learners whose ideas are easily dismissed. Another possibility is that a challenge to their ideas indicates that their colleagues are, indeed, taking them very seriously. Another factor that complicates our understanding of this finding is the degree of autonomy learners feel that they have in performing their duties. The majority of learner-leaders responding to our survey felt that they had a high degree of control over their work and the methods they use to perform their duties. In our short time together, it was not possible to fully explore the meaning behind this conflict. The only lesson we can take away from this discussion is that we need to be cognizant of the perspective of these learner-leaders and the internal conflict they are feeling.

This should not be an excuse to walk on eggshells, nor does it imply that every idea proposed by learner-leaders should be implemented simply because it was proposed by a learner. Even the most vocal spokesperson acknowledged that she needed to learn effective ways to accept criticism. By the same token we all could benefit from improved group decision-making processes.

Recommendations

Based on this very preliminary research, we offer the following recommendations:

1. Compile resources and strategies for meeting staff development needs of learner-leaders. Most programs struggle with budgetary restrictions and, despite the ironic fact that we are in the business of helping others achieve their learning goals, our own professional development often takes a backseat. We recommend additional research into alternative, low-cost resources and strategies. These resources may include case studies, mentors, online training, workshops at regional resource centers, bibliographies, and online databases.

An online database could include the skills and expertise of learner-leaders within a geographic region and facilitate learning across organizations. For example, we have the skeleton of information for such a database. The raw material we collected during the retreat could be refined and structured into an online searchable database of learner-leader resources for California libraries. This process could then be replicated regionally throughout the country and used to identify workshop leaders and to establish learner-to-learner mentoring opportunities. For example, as noted earlier, the duration of employment among learner-leaders at the retreat ranged from three months to eight years. One learner who had been on staff for eight years was often cited as a resource that the other learners had turned to when they had questions or were looking for ideas. As one learner stated, "I don't reinvent anything if I can steal something that's already been done!" Another learner pointed out enthusiastically, "Obviously in this room there's a lot of strength, lots of expertise here. Sometimes we cut ourselves short. Let's get grant money for training amongst ourselves. There is a lot we can do within this group."

2. Conduct national and regional institutes that target learners who are paid staff and their program managers. A number of programs and organizations have leadership training. Literacy Volunteers of America con-

ducts full-day learner-leadership training and recently added the requirement that program managers also attend. The Santa Clara County Library
Reading Program offers a one-year Henry Huffman Leadership Institute,
and the Greater Columbia Literacy Council has leadership training for
learners. However, this training is not focused on learners who are staff.
Existing leadership training should be adapted to focus on learners who
are on staff. We recommend this focus because our interviews revealed
that the transition from volunteer to staff carries a unique set of challenges. As these leaders develop their own skills, they are in an ideal position to share their knowledge with the peers within their own program. A
focus on paid staff may also present an opportunity for a follow-up evaluation that might not be possible with volunteers. We further recommend
that this training result in a certificate that acknowledges their skill attainment and is meaningful to them.

3. Conduct job analyses and translate performance objectives and skills
into Equipped for the Future's (EFF) Four Dimensions of Performance
Language. Approximately one-fourth of the participants are using EFF
standards developed by the National Institute for Literacy in their program.[3] The most common application is during learner intake as a tool for
helping learners identify goals according to the family, community member, and worker role maps. They then use the skills wheel to help incoming learners further refine their own learning plans. One learner who is
well versed in EFF suggested that EFF is a tool that the group could use for
their own goal setting and to identify their group learning needs. Given
their enthusiasm for EFF and their desire to use it in their own personal
development, training them to use the dimensions of performance for
their own self-assessment could result in important research findings for
the field and move EFF toward greater integration into the programs these
learners represent.

We also recommend that programs include personal literacy goals in
performance objectives and reviews. Every learner participating in the
retreat acknowledged an ongoing need for literacy development and a
regret that their jobs have taken precedence over their own literacy goals.
We would argue that continued tutoring is not only in the best interest of
the learner but also has the advantage to the program of keeping the
learner in a position to speak actively. What better way to inspire persistence than for learner-leaders to demonstrate it by continuing to pursue
their own literacy development goals?

4. Establish career paths based on the learner-leader's goals both within
the field of literacy as well as beyond their position as learner-leaders.

A surprising number of these learner-leaders have a desire to become program managers. (Or perhaps it is only surprising to the former program manager involved in this research!) This desire was evident when we initially tallied their requests for additional training and noted that grant writing had a respectable lead over all other tasks. Once they realized how much program managers are called upon to write grants, those who had not previously selected it as a priority changed their minds, making it the only unanimously requested training. One learner issued a passionate plea, "If we learn how to write a grant, it's a way to get services to these people and get money for your job. As I am working, I am putting my mind on the future. I know how to run the program. You can start a program. I don't know what we need. Maybe we need a degree?"

5. Continue research. As noted earlier, our research is very preliminary and has so far only included the perspective of the learners. Since we represent both a learner and a program manager, we realize that this is an incomplete picture. We still need to have a better understanding of the challenges program managers face in bringing learners into positions as paid staff. We have heard war stories of program managers battling bureaucracies in order to hire learners whose duties and skills do not fit rigid civil service definitions. For example, learners complained about the low pay, the lack of job security, and the non-benefited contract nature of their positions. Ironically, a transcript of this conversation could almost be a "word-processed cut and paste" of conversations taking place among all literacy program staff. Future research could focus on determining if there is a disparity between the salary and job status of learners versus other program staff. An executive position does not necessarily mean that the program manager has any autonomy or decision-making authority over hiring, salary, and benefits. Even program managers who have a high degree of autonomy could benefit from job templates and skill indicators that they could use for hiring, setting salaries, and determining staff development needs.

Truly Learner-Centered

If literacy programs are going to be truly "learner-centered," then the learners in those programs must have a strong voice and take on leadership roles. This goal is widely embraced by library literacy programs. However, too little is known about how to implement this goal and the barriers that prevent greater involvement of learners as equal partners in program development. Anne Serino (Lynn, Mass.) noted in a National Literacy Advocacy (NLA) electronic discussion dated March 11, 2000, "Leaders emerge, but leadership skills need to be nurtured and taught. . . . I know that it is not easy to implement and sustain student leadership development. It means we have to learn new ways of leading our organizations, develop new skills and share authority. Student leadership initiatives require time, energy, commitment, resources, and patience."

We are a long way from fully understanding how to achieve this goal, but we believe that we as a field are making important strides and have a rough draft of an action plan for further research and discussion.

Emma Torrez's Story

Torrez is a learner advocate for the Santa Clara City Library Literacy Program and the Santa Clara County Library Reading Program. She is a frequently requested workshop leader and a board member for VALUE, a national board of adult literacy students.

"Five years ago I went to the LVA Conference and one of the workshops was about a statewide Learners' Council. I thought that it was such a very good idea. I went back to our program and talked to my program director and to the Learners' Council at the Santa Clara County Library Reading Program. For the next 5 years we talked about having a retreat for adult learners who are on staff. About 3 months ago we called Carole Talan at the California State Library and asked if it was possible. She said "yes" and we were happy that June 23–24, 2000, it came true.

"I got to see and meet 21 adult learners who are on staff at CLC Literacy programs in California, some of whom I knew. To hear the different jobs and tasks that they all do, and the barriers that they face, was so amazing. I knew the job and tasks that I perform were sometimes hard and difficult for me. They are somewhat easier for me now. But some of the learners have only been working for about 9 months. They are just starting out and I know that they are scared. I know where they're coming from. I was scared, too, and I still am sometimes. This was a chance for me to tell them I've been there, too. I know how they feel.

"Some said that they need more training for their jobs and some need more help. Sometimes I still do, too. I can go to staff in our program and ask for help and get it. I know that having a adult learner on staff is very important for a literacy program, but I think there needs to be a massive training for all adults coming on to staff. This is a good start!"

NOTES

1. Our work thus far has focused on documenting the learners' perspectives and to develop recommendations for their professional development. We believe this focus will result in action plans the field can begin to implement immediately. We recognize that program managers face enormous obstacles to hiring (budgetary restrictions, civil service employment requirements, etc.) and to supporting learners on staff. These challenges need to be documented and studied in order to complete the picture.

2. While the job titles varied from office clerk to workplace literacy coordinator to student advocate, we will use the term learner-leader for simplicity and because it captures the role each of these participants fill in their programs.

3. See www.nifl.gov.

■ 6 ■

Whole Literacy in Plymouth

Literacy as a Library Service

DINAH L. O'BRIEN

We know the statistics; we know the buzzwords, the current "catchy" trends: TQM; staff empowerment; customers, not patrons. A redesigned planning process has begun to alter the way traditional public library services are developed and delivered. We will not broach on the automation revolution, begun in the '80s and still evolving. Full text has replaced journal citations, online databases have resulted in cost shifting of resources, current information is available instantly through the Internet instead of the next press run, and our card catalog cabinets, long replaced with computer terminals, are showing up at yard sales, redesigned as tchotchkes with an antique flair.

Through it all, libraries, librarians, support staff, and funding agencies have made one underlying assumption: that all these wonderful things are accessible to all customers. Moreover, where we have realized that accessibility is not universal, we have gone to great expense to alter physical structures, provide audio assistance for the vision impaired, compensated for the deaf, and developed extensive programs for the infirm. However, even through these worthwhile and necessary endeavors, we have made an assumption that can undo all the good. We assume that everyone over the age of 10 can read English at least on a fifth-grade level. They cannot.

UNESCO reports that as we enter the new millennium, approximately 26.9 percent of the adult population is illiterate. Between 5 and 20 percent of adults in industrialized nations are functionally illiterate. UNESCO describes functional literacy as the ability of a person to "engage in all those activities in which literacy is required for effective functioning of his group and community and also for enabling him to continue to use reading, writing and calculation for his own and the community's development."[1] In a country where the public school systems permeate to the smallest hamlet, where trillions of tax dollars are provided to the next generation for their development and education, where institutions of higher learning are revered and respected, we are consistently troubled by that portion of our population deemed functionally illiterate. We expend much time, energy, and money to correct this inequity in our larger urban centers and major cities. However, in middle and small-town America we often adopt the NIMBY ("not in my backyard") stance and remain unaware of a population left unserved. In our urban areas, small cities, and towns, that greatest resource for adult basic education is the public library. Moreover, it is through the public library and its community involvement and staff commitment that change happens in so many lives.

Community Needs

Where is the local public library to begin? In Plymouth, Massachusetts, it began the way all library initiatives begin, with community analysis. In the late 1980s, inspired by the Bush administration's goals for adult literacy, Plymouth, a town of approximately 50,000 located in southeastern Massachusetts, began working with nine other local communities on the literacy issue. Statistics were gathered from state and local databases concerning educational achievement in the area. Data sources included unemployment statistics, local dropout rates, anecdotal information gathered from personal interviews, and supplemental data from the Commonwealth Literacy Campaign. A collaborative effort was launched consisting of business, government, school, and library staff as well as community members. Library Services and Construction Act (LSCA) funds were awarded and the Literacy Program of Greater Plymouth was off and running. Tutor recruitment and training were held at the Plymouth Public Library on a biannual basis. Tutors and learners used library space for meetings. A fledgling literacy collection of materials was purchased, cataloged, and shelved in a "literacy nook" for specialized and general usage. Fund-raising events were held, advertising was published, and collaborative relationships were developed. Later the program also turned to the Massachusetts Department of Education for additional program support and was awarded a five-year grant to support a newly developed GED program to complement the one-on-one, federally funded tutoring. Nearly 400 adult learners passed through the program.

This good thing came to a near screeching halt with the demise of LSCA in the mid-'90s. The governing collaboration had been waning for some time, with Plymouth still providing space and staff support. With the termination of federal funds came the real danger of losing state funds. Coalitions developed and expanded with local Head Start programs providing classroom space and child care; CURA, a local visiting nurse service offering health care advice to students; and local women's shelters offering support and assistance where needed. All were consulted for solutions. All offered support and encouragement but were involved in their own missions and could not lead.

The Library Board was beginning its update of the Pubic Library Planning Process, and along with staff, town officials, and the community, was in the analysis phase. Staff began surveying library customers. The town's Planning, School, Building, and Council on Aging Departments were interviewed and statistical information gathered. The Board of Trustees arranged for community members to be interviewed about their perceptions of and expectations for library services. Four areas were clearly identified: Reference and Resource Center, Preschool Door to Learning, Community Information Center, and Formal Education Support Center. Existing library programs were evaluated, adjusted, rated, and energized. Area 4, Formal Education Support Center, was of special interest. The library has a strong history in this area through active youth/reference department coordination with area schools. The Library Corporation also owns the building used by a local community college. This was a "plug-in" location for the existing literacy program. However, with the financial changes afoot, it was now time to evaluate the library and community's commitment to adult literacy.

Through several successful LSCA grants and the planning process, the need for literacy service was clearly established and documented. In fact, a successful program has been in place for six years. The library involvement has been "host" and lead grant signatory for the effort. There was a generic job description on file with the Town Personnel Department that covered all grant-funded town positions. The town treasurer managed grant funds, the literacy coordinator reported to an independent, unrecognized volunteer board with the assistant library director attending monthly meetings. Clients accessed the service through direct contact with the literacy office and the program was advertised through various avenues and agencies.

As the worlds collided, passing of LSCA and completion of the planning process, it became obvious that changes had to be made. But was the commitment there on the part of the community and library to take a program someone else was paying for and adopt it as their own? Armed with the community analysis, statistics, and documented success, the first stop was the library director's office. The director is responsible to the community for library services, and it was clear that the community thought literacy was on a par with adult and youth services. Both reference and storytime are traditionally associated with public libraries, both based on the assumption of literacy. How do you start a library-based program based on English as a second language, nonreading or inadequate skills, and learning disabilities? Can an existing literacy program be integrated into traditional library services? Through a customer-service-based program it can. By reviewing youth services it was learned that family literacy was already a concern and was being addressed in preliminary ways. The Reference Department was already establishing basic information and referral with the Literacy Program of Greater Plymouth and other sources, but it was not considered on a routine basis. Circulation was only mentioning literacy services in passing with new patrons. Little or no readers' advisory services were performed at the basic literacy level. Customers were asking for the service, but it was not fully accepted as anything other than a temporary grant position by staff. That became the starting point.

Community Desires

After consultation with, and approval by, the Board of Library Trustees, the director's office began intensive work on customer service with the staff. Total Quality groups were begun involving all staff, including the grant-funded literacy coordinator. The coordinator was invited to attend library staff meetings, report as a department head at meetings, and participate in collection development discussions. Monthly reports of the Literacy Program of Greater Plymouth were also delivered to the Library Board of Trustees at their regular meeting; a trustee was appointed as literacy liaison. The coordinator paired with other staff to promote library services throughout the community. Before long, and through osmosis, the program began to become an integral part of customer services in the minds of staff. Information and referral increased, the coordinator both consulted with and was consulted by other staff for projects, and community outreach increased. Approximately 10 percent of referrals were now coming from the circulation desk. Training in active listening skills and skilled communication were paying off for customers. Staff morale rose in all departments and patron satisfaction with service increased.

The second step to total program integration was acceptance by the governing authority. Job descriptions for both union and nonunion staff were being reevaluated by the Personnel Department. The existing general grant employee description was reworked to reflect the library's need for a new professional position. A critical decision was made at that point that a professional educator, *not* a professional librarian, was needed to manage the department. As Christine Watkins pointed out in her *American Libraries* article "Chapter Report: The State Literacy Scene," "Traditionally, libraries have served a reading public. But as libraries have become increasingly involved in the literacy movement, they have had to learn new ways of thinking about library services."[2] The model job description was therefore not a librarian but that of a curriculum coordinator in the local school department. The completed new and revised descriptions, approved by the staff and the Board of Library Trustees, were then presented to Town Meeting for approval. Hurdle two was successfully removed, but there was still no funding.

The next progression into a whole library-based literacy program was actually funding the position through the governing authority. This was painful, exhausting, and exhilarating.

In New England, the Town Meeting is still the final authority, and convincing 104 Town Meeting members is no small feat, even with support of

A further indication of the way adult literacy activities are imbedded in the fabric of library services is the source of funding. Although many literacy activities may have been spurred by grant funding, more than half (57.6%) of revenue spent on literacy activities (in the most recently completed fiscal year) came from libraries' recurring annual operating budget, that is, local taxes. Only 10.9% was received from state aid, 9.3% from donations and gifts, 6.9% from non-library foundation grants and 6.3% from federal government grants. *Survey,* p. 14

the selectmen, town manager, and Finance Committee. Discussion was all over the map: outlines of the program and community needs, testimonial from willing students, concern that literacy was the responsibility of the School Department, denial of the problem, and, finally, acknowledgment of the need but decision to allocate limited resources elsewhere. With each defeat, the commitment of the library grew stronger. It took two annual meetings before acceptance, but by then there was unanimous consent. The Literacy Program of Greater Plymouth was now a funded part of the Library Department, complete with salary, supplies, and materials. The LSCA funding expired that spring.

With this victory, the stage has been set for some fantastic work! In the planning process an objective was to "provide for continued accessibility of adult literacy classes which shall include, but not be limited to GED, ESL instruction" with a goal of establishing the staff position by 1995—we were off by two years.[3] The library mission statement says in part, "The mission of the Plymouth Public Library is to select, acquire, organize, preserve and make conveniently accessible services and a collection of materials in various formats held in common by the people of Plymouth for the *educational,* cultural, recreational and informational needs and interests. The library is an agent for all citizens in securing needed information and materials without bias or censorship."[4] Literacy fits the bill along with traditional services. We have been able to establish stronger collaborative ties with other local service agencies with the strength of the municipal government behind the program. When additional classroom space was required, the town provided the space, something not done under grant funding. The relationship with the local community college has led to a grand opportunity for Literacy Program of Greater Plymouth GED graduates—a guaranteed seat in either the two-year associates degree program or the certificate program, students' choice.

Staff involvement has also expanded. Through training, continuing education, and counseling, the professional and nonprofessional staff of the library no longer simply give lip service to their support of the literacy component. Programs are developed with literacy goals in mind; the library brochure generated for new customers includes a literacy flyer. Tours are provided for new students; bibliographic instruction is included in the curriculum. Publicity is handled through the development coordinator's office, which now also solicits funds for the program. The Board of Library Trustees manages trust funds, and the unrecognized independent literacy board now serves as an adjunct advisor to the program.

The library collection is incorporating materials that may be of interest to literacy students. The "literacy nook" is currently being reorganized and weeded. Cataloging is being updated. The YA collection is being used to supplement the literacy nook with high-interest/low-vocabulary materials shelved in both the adult and youth departments. With the coordinator attending collection development meetings, the alignment between classroom and collection support becomes a seamless process.

To Satisfy the Need

Make no mistake, none of this has been easy. Librarians are sometimes not exactly the welcoming type and libraries can be intimidating places for the nonreader. Traditionally, teaching people to read has been the responsibility of the school system or volunteers from social service agencies. While we do not mind teaching children how to read in our storytime environment, we have not adopted the same fervor with the adult population. Librarians have also spent considerable time emphasizing the importance of the MLS in library work; we are slow, or unwilling, to accept as "colleague" a non-MLS person working side by side us in a library. Issues such as pay scale, union membership, professional responsibilities, office space, and funding become points of contention. The correlation between teaching children to read and teaching adults to read seems to have passed over library school education. And it is in this setting that we are trying to make the library experience for nonreaders fruitful and exciting?

What do we need to do to make our libraries literacy-friendly? First, we need to offer some sort of literacy training in our library schools, not education courses, but at the very least graduate students should attend a basic literacy volunteer training session to become familiar with the process. It is this training, the basic backbone of adult literacy programs, that can open a world of possibilities for library staff. It is in training sessions that we will learn what tutors and learners need to know about the library, how they feel about our services, and what we can do to make the literacy experience beneficial to all. They will tell us how to be welcoming and what we can do to meet their needs. We afforded the physically challenged this luxury, why not the reading challenged?

In training sessions, librarians can also assist tutors and learners in learning the ways of the library. What exactly can librarians do for customers, what ma'   .ls are available, and what services do we offer? For many individuals, the public library is a representative of government structure that is exclusionary. This concept must be changed; comfort levels need to be established. Video tours of the library on local cable channels as well as tape must be available. Audio tours on tape are great ways to integrate library services into conversational ESL. Rewording standard library brochures and handouts into a high-interest/low-vocabulary format will truly make the information available to all. Look at the library collection as well as the literacy collection, and make sure they contain complementary workbooks, ESL conversation materials, dictionaries, grammar, hi/low leisure and nonfiction materials. Encourage customers to use the entire collection; there might be tutors out there who stumble upon materials and gain an interest they never knew they had. And do not assume that tutors know how to use the library. How many people do you know, other than librarians, who remember how to make use of all the wonderful resources available to them after they have written that last paper and graduated?

In closing I would like to share with you what the Plymouth Public Library, in addition to the above suggestions, is doing to promote whole-library literacy and learner retention. With the assistance of the Lila Wallace-Reader's Digest Fund, a literacy technology-training lab has been constructed. It is used by learners to encourage conversation, improve listening skills, and develop computer skills that may be used on the job, in daily life, or to improve writing. All of this is aimed at learners' retention in a literacy program to ensure that they meet their goals. At the same time, library staff participates in lab development, machine maintenance, and collection development. It is hoped that general library customers who read and hear about the lab will want to become tutors, the general library will use learner skills, and library staff will provide some instruction in technology/Internet use. The lab, while not the whole, is a vital part in our continued quest for a whole-library based adult literacy program in Plymouth, Massachusetts.

NOTES

1. UNESCO *Courier* (May 1990), pp. 7–8.
2. Christine Watkins, "Chapter Report: The State Library Scene (Role of State Library Associations in Literacy Campaigns)," *American Libraries* 28, 5 (May 1997): 10.
3. Plymouth Public Library Long Range Plan, 1994–1999.
4. Plymouth Public Library Mission Statement, Town of Plymouth, Massachusetts.

▪ 7 ▪

Literacy, Diversity, and Learners

LYNNE A. PRICE

I often think I am the luckiest person around. I love what I do, the people I work with, and the learners I meet who make what I do worthwhile. Working with adult learners is a truly satisfying experience. Oh yes, they have problems in life, things they want to accomplish, and goals they would like to meet, which is just where literacy plays a major role.

Pair Reviews: An Educational Journey

Here at PROJECT READ (the adult literacy program of the San Francisco Public Library), part of the learners' educational journey is meeting for pair reviews. Pair reviews are informal meetings conducted on a quarterly basis to maintain contact with a learner and tutor once they are matched. As instruction supervisor, I am able to monitor the learners' progress and offer additional assistance, resources, and learning strategies to both learner and tutor in these meetings.

Progress is evident as a result of interviewing the pair and reviewing the learner's binder. The binder is a notebook that all learners receive when they come to PROJECT READ for their initial interview and assessment. The binder is divided into three sections: goals, working papers, and portfolio. Learner goals are identified and written at the initial assessment. All work done by the learner is filed in the "working papers" section, and the pieces they feel best exemplify their progress are placed in the "portfolio" section of the binder. This allows learners and tutors to capture the success they may achieve—and they determine what makes a piece a benchmark of progress. Every learner is different, and each works at different levels.

After each review, I give or mail a gift of a book to the learner, basing the selection on their areas of interest. For tutors, I ply them with resources: flashcards, workbooks, handouts. I conduct one-on-one sessions with individuals to teach additional strategies, or give them hands-on exercises. We also offer bimonthly tutor workshops that cover areas of interest and concern to tutors (spelling, phonics, strategies for beginning/intermediate/advanced learners, etc.).

While I can't say that every pair enrolled in our program comes in to the meetings, most do. It's great observing them as they depart a review: there is often a new sense of direction, and a realization of achievements (however large or small) and goals. They walk away with new ideas, a fresh perspective, or realizations in the form of "a-ha!" moments.

One Pair, One Example

Currently there are about 145 pairs working in the program, so the need to monitor and assist is great. Here's a snapshot of one pair.

Tutor Gary and learner Alex are a new team; they were paired together in late March 2000. A former gang member, 20-year-old Alex began taking drugs and drinking at 11 years of age and graduated to snorting heroin. He presently is in recovery and very proud of his progress so far: "No one made me come. I realized I needed this myself—and for myself."

As we sat together and reviewed his progress, we discussed the ways in which progress was taking place. Gary was like a proud parent as he discussed the changes in Alex. "He's constantly evolving. He's timely for every session, and comes prepared to work." This was a step Alex had chosen to take, and he received an immediate sense of satisfaction as he really reviewed his work of the past few months. Change was already evident—in his word recognition and the writing assignments he worked at completing.

The homework topic is one that crops up constantly in these meetings. The one area in which Gary struggles is in helping Alex acknowledge the importance of doing work outside of their sessions. We discussed the importance of working independently. Many times learners try to depend solely on the work done in sessions with their tutors, not grasping the importance of practice done between sessions. Analogies of golf, weight training, and other sports help Alex sense the need for repetition in his meetings with Gary, and the idea of getting a better "workout" in between their sessions.

Gary and Alex meet together twice weekly for two hours per session. They felt their sessions together go really well. "I study so many things now. I notice and read signs around the city, notices posted in the home where I stay, and feel better reading the material I have to cover in my program." Gary also mentioned how well the sessions were progressing: "Alex knows a lot, and really works at getting better in every session. He's not as shy as he was in the beginning, and is beginning to take more risks in his reading and writing."

One of my favorite points to make with learners is the importance of taking risks, and that reading and writing are the best risks they may ever take. "There are no word police to say you're incorrect—your session is the safest place to experience being right or wrong."

One area Alex experiences frustration in is his spelling. Many learners will neglect writing for this very reason! They also seem to believe they are the only poor spellers known to humankind. Once we discuss that this is a global problem, and they don't have a corner on the market, they often ease up on themselves, and commit to doing some writing. I encourage them to start small, a sentence or paragraph at a time, and work their way up. They are also encouraged to do free writing that is not critiqued by the tutor, but is used as a vehicle to simply get them more comfortable and confident with the writing process. As this type of writing continues, the learner often is able to move into grammar, punctuation, and spelling omissions with greater ease. The free writing may take the form of the learner writing in a journal, or as a joint exercise with the learner and tutor. As a joint exercise, the tutor is not to critique or correct the work but allow for dialogue to be written, and write in a way to encourage the learner to respond in kind. This part of the session is not lost on Alex; he begins to identify how much writing plays a part in his learning process as we review his initial goals—almost all contain the need to write. The "a-ha" moment for Alex has arrived. "I can't do what I really want to do without working at my writing. I hate how it looks and the fact that a lot of my words are spelled wrong, but I know too, that I just got to keep practicing, practicing at it until I am satisfied."

I look forward to meeting with Alex and Gary again in three months. At that point, we will review goals and progress, administer assessments to capture same, and celebrate Alex's achievements once again.

Cultural Diversity in Literacy Programs

Over the past several years there has been a continual and growing discussion with respect to cultural diversity. One segment is taking place within literacy circles. These discussions, which can be read in online discussion lists, take place among participants and staff, and are reiterated in summit meetings. Within the American Library Association (ALA), Cultural Diversity Fairs at annual conferences allow participants nationwide to view how diversity is being addressed within libraries and literacy programs. Workshops and task forces at ALA annual conferences address the importance of diversity in literacy programs, with a hope of encouraging dialogues to continue on a global scale.

The yearly reports, grant proposals, information packets for donors, and other documentation support the importance of recognizing the populations literacy programs work so hard to assist. But diversity covers more than the participants; it speaks to the need for review and constant enhancement on the part of programs and those who support them.

When I became more familiar with the many literacy programs within the state of California as well as around the country, and the work they do with their participants, the phrase "cultural diversity" took on a broader scope. I could no longer view as a personal need my desire to make an impact within my program and on other programs. We are accustomed to a diverse group of learners, but diversity speaks to population, areas of need, manners in which needs are recognized and addressed.

In discussions, this is a subject that can spark debate and a range of emotions. Often discussions simply cease instead of addressing crucial questions such as: how much more can we discuss this? What else should we do? Is it about being politically correct, or do we really delve into the concerns that the topic suggests? Do we really explore what program participants voice as their concerns? Do we examine what staff view as their concerns?

We need to weave discussions of diversity into our ongoing conversations about literacy.

- We recognize the concept is not just a buzzword for the new millennium.
- We realize we are not all equal but should have equal opportunity.
- We create opportunities for discussions to take place.
- We take and make the opportunities as we see them.
- We decline being a victim but advocate in positive and growing ways.

I realize that my desires and dreams are not mine alone—many more people that I am aware of share them. But if we are the voices of our community, we must continue and expand the work that we do, working for all, in every manner we can envision. In California, cultural diversity has been expanded into a working group. Within the California Literacy Campaign, a committee was formed in 1999 to discuss and collectively research ways for cultural diversity to continue expanding within the California literacy programs. While we have a vision of what we as literacy programs can do, this vision constantly changes. It's one that becomes difficult to fit into time frames of when a particular task is done, or the goal is completed. The list of tasks seems to evolve. I believe each committee member sees this as work in progress, as one that will—and should rightfully so—be ongoing. We discussed reviving the Ethnic Tutor Campaign throughout California; we have surveyed library literacy programs as to the needs of tutors, learners, staff, and materials. We hope to build a Diversity toolbook that can be used by programs. At our last meeting, we discussed the hopes of the committee; this was translated in the form of an ever-growing mission statement (please note that this is not a final draft).

We hope to:

- bring visibility and awareness to the issue of diversity
- define diversity as it relates to library literacy programs
- ensure that all members of the adult community who were not served well by the K–12 system or missed their childhood educational development because of location, illness, or work are assured of the opportunity to have access to free mentoring support to get lifelong learning
- help prepare the CLC for the future in California
- develop a process and products that help literacy programs implement diversity on many levels in their programs
- increase sensitivity in the literacy community to the various aspects of diversity including, but not limited to, gender, race, ethnicity, age, and ability.

It may not be all that we can do, but the discussion continues. Let's all keep taking steps to ensure that cultural diversity is at the heart of our programs.

▪ 8 ▪

Project READ

Redwood City Public Library

KATHY ENDAYA

The Redwood City Public Library Project READ Program is a free, volunteer-based literacy program for adults, children, and families who want to improve their literacy skills. Four complementary literacy programs are offered to fill the literacy needs of the community, and are supported by the generous help of our volunteers.

Project READ's four program service areas are:

Adult Literacy—A one-to-one or small-group instruction model providing individualized literacy tutoring for adults who read below the seventh-grade level.

Families for Literacy—A home- or library-based literacy program for parents and their preschool-aged children. Parents meet one-to-one or in small groups with their tutors.

Families in Partnership Program—A dropout prevention program offering one-to-one tutoring for first- through eighth-grade children.

Kids in Partnership Program—A one-to-one after-school dual intervention program that matches academically at-risk teen tutors with academically at-risk elementary students.

Learning gains of all Project READ participants are regularly monitored, primarily through formal reading/language assessment, attitude and behavior inventories, oral reading skills, and telephone conferences.

Project READ cooperates extensively with local public schools in serving children and families; some referrals are made by social services and private industry. Redwood City Friends of Literacy (RCFOL), a nonprofit fundraising board, hopes to amass enough political and financial support for Project READ to continue to meet the literacy needs of the community.

The Community

Redwood City, located on the San Francisco Peninsula midway between San Francisco and San José, is a diverse, rapidly changing community of some 76,000 residents. In Redwood City, named for the redwood trees shipped from its port during the 1800s to build San Francisco, affluent families live in the hills, while those with low incomes live closer to the port. Middle-class housing is situated between these two extremes.

Hispanics make up about one-fourth of the area's population, having doubled their numbers during the 1980s. Currently more than half of all public elementary school children are Hispanic. A significant segment of Redwood City's Hispanic community has roots in a single town in Mexico, where educational opportunities were extremely limited. It is therefore hardly surprising that those who come to Project READ, on average, read at a second- to third-grade level, even though they may have been in the United States for decades.

The Library

Across the street from the new City Hall sits the public library, a handsome and functional 1988 conversion of an old fire station. Two small branch libraries provide neighborhood-based services, one catering primarily to Hispanic families. Project READ is located on the second floor of the main library branch.

Project READ

Literacy programming at Redwood City Public Library (RCPL) grew out of informal links with neighborhood literacy programs in San Mateo and Menlo Park, to which all local inquiries were being referred. In early 1986, a Redwood City staff member interested in literacy was granted five hours per week to initiate services by interviewing and matching students with tutors trained by the other literacy programs. At the same time, all library staff participated in a seminar on literacy services designed to increase their awareness of the needs of adults with low literacy and to learn how to provide referral information.

A committed staff member, supported by the library director, pressed for a full-blown literacy program within RCPL. Perhaps the turning point came at a meeting in late 1986 at which an adult literacy student spoke. A longtime library board member, brought to the meeting by the librarian, describes that as the moment at which he became committed to a literacy program and began to solicit the support of other board members. "Before that," he said, "I was against it. There was no space, inadequate facilities, no money." In April 1987, RCPL submitted a proposal to the State Library, seeking California Literacy Campaign funds to establish an adult literacy program, and in September of that year the library was awarded a California Library Service Act (CLSA) five-year grant. Project READ was born.

A project director, without formal library training, was recruited to implement Project READ. From the outset, three literacy staff positions were built into the library's operating budget. When another FTE was subsequently added, it too was incorporated into the library budget, with the result that these positions are no more vulnerable to fiscal cutbacks than other positions in the library.

By September 1988, a year after receiving funding, an adult literacy program was well established, with approximately 60 student/tutor pairs meeting weekly. Roughly based on the Literacy Volunteers of America model, the adult literacy program continues to be the largest Project READ component. Tutors receive 12 hours of basic tutor training, followed by 3 hours of specialized training if they choose to work with Families for Literacy (FFL) or the Families in Partnership Program (FIPP). The teen tutors attend special training preparing them to work in the Kids in Partnership Program (KIP).

Ongoing supervision and technical assistance is provided by Project READ staff, who encourage the tutors to tailor literacy instruction to the needs and interests of their students by making use of the library materials and special literacy program resources. Tutors, as well as potential literacy students, are asked to make, at minimum, a six-month commitment before joining. Most tutoring occurs at the library (usually in an out-of-the-way area near the literacy program office) or at one of the library branches, community centers, or a church. FFL tutoring takes place at the homes of tutors and students, or at the library. School sites are meeting places for small-group instruction. The children of the parents meeting in small groups attend Kids Literacy Club: a program developed to provide preschool activities and homework assistance for the children.

Families for Literacy

In 1989, Project READ added an additional literacy component, the Families for Literacy (FFL) Program. Initially funded through another CLSA grant, FFL was designed to serve a difficult-to-reach population, which is referred through elementary schools and preschools—namely, families with preschoolers or kindergarten children with at least one parent reading at less than a seventh-grade level.

FFL has adopted a three-phase approach. In the first phase, the family and tutor meet at the family's home. During this phase the tutor and parent(s) negotiate learning goals that include reading with their preschoolers. In the second phase, the family is introduced to the library through an informal tour conducted by the tutor, with whom a relationship has already been firmly established. This leads to the third phase of the program, in which tutoring continues at home, and a parent and the young children are invited to attend regularly scheduled story hours at the library with their tutor. The FFL program currently serves 60 families in the one-on-one tutoring model and 54 families in the small-group tutoring model.

Families in Partnership Program

In 1990, Project READ added the Families in Partnership Program (FIPP) to serve children in grades 1 through 8 who may be at risk of dropping out of school. Potential students are identified by public school teachers and staff, but parental approval and support are required before matching the youths with tutors. Students attend two tutoring sessions per week. FIPP tutors and their students use materials appropriate to the child's interest and reading level. Although these are intended to meet the student's academic needs, they are not school-based materials. Rather, because FIPP strives to instill youth with a love of learning, a fundamental premise of materials selection is that children will read what is interesting to them and will be more likely to read in the future if they find the process enjoyable. Tutors are encouraged to use the library as a resource; Project READ provides books, magazines, and instructional materials; and technical assistance is available to them from the Project READ staff, the library staff, and school district personnel.

Student Assessment

Project READ regularly assesses learning gains. As part of the intake process, entering students in all programs are given the Bader Reading and Language Assessment Inventory, an open-ended assessment that requires 10 to 30 minutes to administer, depending upon the reading skills of the student. The assessment is presented as an opportunity for staff to determine which books tutors should begin with, and to ensure that no false assumptions are made about the students' abilities that might unintentionally result in feelings of boredom or frustration. Although not required, it is expected that students be reassessed every six months for as long as they remain in Project READ or achieve a twelfth-grade reading level.

Students and tutors also complete pre- and post-program attitudinal and behavioral inventories that assess student and family reading habits and library use, as well as estimates of the child's reading awareness, attitudes towards the library story hour component of the program, and oral language development, customer satisfaction, and suggestions on future services offered by the program.

After trying numerous reporting/monitoring systems, Project READ staff have settled on a routine of phoning both students and tutors on a regular basis, contacting one of the pair every month. From these calls, staff are able to obtain an accurate measure of which pairs are meeting, how often, and what learning issues they are currently dealing with. The phone conversations also serve as an opportunity to troubleshoot, to pass on new information, or to make suggestions for additional or different tutorial materials. When difficulties arise within student/tutor pairs, Project READ staff help to resolve the problems. Staff encourage students and tutors to call the office to brainstorm solutions with the program coordinator.

Collaborative Partnerships

Project READ coordinates its services with numerous human service providers in the area. For example, ESL students are referred to Project READ, particularly those who might benefit most from individual tutoring. The Private Industry Council, Regional Occupational Program (ROP), and Canada College refer students to Project READ for literacy tutoring, while Project READ refers students to these collaborative partners for benefit from job training. In addition, Project READ disseminates information related to community service organizations and employers within the Redwood City area, and serves as linking mechanism for promoting increased cooperation and support.

Extensive cooperation occurs between Project READ and the public elementary schools, with school staff making themselves available for consultation with literacy tutors, and frequently referring parents to the Families for Literacy and Families in Partnership Programs. They also invite Project READ staff to attend meetings to exchange information about the elementary school children attending the Kids in Partnership tutoring sessions.

Funding

Through the support of the Library Board and City Council, the RCPL has sought to include the staff as regular city employees whenever possible. Yet funding issues remain a necessary preoccupation of the Project READ director. The program established a nonprofit 501(c)3 organization, the Redwood City Friends of Literacy (RCFOL), with the goal of raising the necessary funds to support the Project READ programs through fund-raising, higher awareness, and grant funding. It is also hoped that the RCFOL will amass sufficient clout to secure continued political and financial support for the program. Project READ's long-term objective is to secure enough funding to allow the program to expand and change in the future to meet the needs of the community.

Local Library Facts

Location: Urban-Suburban

Branches: 2

Literacy Program Established: 1987

Project READ Clientele

Clients Currently Served	350
LEP (Limited English Proficient) Clients	30%

Racial/Ethnic Composition:

African American	8%
Asian	9%
Hispanic/Latino	55%
Native American	3%
White	21%
Other	4%

Lee Walls's Story

I knew that I couldn't read. And one day I was filling out an application for a job interview. Once I got past the door she was interviewing me and she had me read a paragraph and I couldn't get through it so she recommended Project READ. I thought to myself that its time that I take care of the problem that I had. I remember thinking on my way down to the Project READ office of how good it would be to be able to read. I came right on down because there had been so many years that I had just skated by, getting jobs, not knowing how to read.

I was nervous when I got there but she was so nice, her name was Margaret. I thought that everyone would be looking at me because I couldn't read but she made me feel comfortable, she said I did alright on the test. She said not to worry about it that it wasn't really a test. She just set me up right there and told me when I could start with a tutor. She didn't hesitate.

I had been going through life without reading and I didn't want anyone to find out that I couldn't read, that's including family members and friends. And then I finally just said "I need help." I always wanted to read but I fell behind in the 5th grade and never caught up. And I tried to catch up too. I remember in the 8th grade they had a new program with tapes and a headset and I tried that but it didn't work. So I kind of covered it up. Then you fall so far behind you feel you'll never catch up. So I got into drugs and alcohol. This continued for fifteen years. It seems like it was longer.

I grew up in Memphis, Tennessee. It was a projects-type environment and most of the things around me was drugs and alcohol. I started drinking in the sixth grade and doing drugs. I made it all the way through the 11th grade. Teachers just let me pass. My drug addiction got so bad that I wasn't there most of the time. The only reason I dropped out was because the principal came across me and said "You haven't been here in two months, why don't you drop out!" And I said "No problem." It is so easy for people who can't read to say 'no problem' because they don't want to deal with it anyway. You try to sweep it under the rug. That's exactly what I tried to do all those years, sweep it under the rug.

Now I have a dream of doing something. Before I was limited by reading abilities. It just limited me to certain jobs, certain things that I could do. And now I have dreams of being a restaurant owner. In the beginning I didn't have those dreams. I see all kinds of changes . . . and everyone around me believes in me. . . . I think I am a lot different now because before I was a lot shyer and wouldn't say anything because I was afraid that people would find out my secret. I was afraid they would treat me different. I always kind of kept to myself and tried not to get around lots of people. So its a lot different now with me. My life has changed because of Project READ and I feel that if a lot of people who can read volunteer as a tutor it would help a lot of people. And as soon as I feel that I'm ready I'm becoming a tutor because of a book I read. The book is called *Each One Teach One.* It was the first book I read.

If there are other people who are out there thinking about volunteering I would like to tell them not to hesitate and to get in there and help someone because there's a lot of adults out there that can not read and it might be a family member that can't read and you wouldn't know because we have a tendency to hide it because we're ashamed of not being able to read. Give someone a dream. A little hope in their life to strive to be the best they can.

I'm an assistant teacher at my church and bible school and I am currently studying to get my GED. Being able to pick up a newspaper or pick up a magazine or to read my own words right now makes me confident. I wouldn't trade this for nothing in the world.

▪ 9 ▪
A Rural Public
Library Literacy Program

KONNI P. CLAYTON

This is the story of how one rural public library started a literacy program in a small community in east central Illinois. It is a simple story, but one with great impact. This story can be translated into an action plan for other rural communities interested in starting a literacy program, and for existing literacy providers desiring to improve their services. Before telling the *how* of this tale, it is beneficial to know the *why* of it.

Why Literacy in Rural Public Libraries?

Rural public libraries serve millions of Americans, frequently serving both as a community center and as a main access point for knowledge. While patron portraits often include commonalities, rural public libraries serve every race, social class, religion, and profession. As suburbs extend their boundaries, rural public libraries continue to experience increased patron diversity. In President Bill Clinton's second State of the Union address, he urged for more "opportunities for every American family," and focused attention on "preparing a public for technology." The president also identified libraries as potential providers for these nationwide tasks.

In creating opportunities for *every* American family, we must include rural families, where equal access to equal opportunities is an issue. Literacy programs funded in libraries bring equal access to citizens where opportunities are often limited by the distance people live from larger cities, where dollars tend to be most generously allocated.

When preparing a public for technology, rural communities represent unique needs. Rural citizens must prepare when learning opportunities present themselves, as opportunities for technology training, advancement, and even exposure to technology are sometimes limited. To truly prepare a population for technology in an equal and effective way, technology opportunities need to be more readily available (i.e., through public libraries where there is equal and fair access) as do opportunities to learn (literacy programs) about the use of technologies.

Another point when considering the significance of library-based literacy programs in rural communities is the influx of immigrants in America since 1978. In the May 23, 2000, issue of *USA Today* we read: "No longer are the nation's 31 million Hispanics concentrated in towns along the U.S. border or in large urban hubs of California, Texas, Florida, and New York. Over the past two decades, tens of thousands of immigrants from Central and South America and Mexico have moved into small towns of rural America. This increasingly diverse population has revamped nearly every aspect of American life: the workplace, grocery store, radio dial, voting booth, and classroom."

English as a Second Language (ESL) instruction is one of the fastest growing needs in rural communities. Library-based literacy programs can provide cost-effective, productive services and resources for addressing these needs. Public libraries stand at the place in a community "where information, reading, the basic tools, and the electronic future meet in a place that belongs to all the people." (See DeCandido, p. 168) Rural public library-based literacy programs stand at the place in America where "equal access" can attain its true meaning.

Our Rural Public Library District

Robinson Public Library District's (RPLD) geographic service area includes sections of western Crawford County, located 240 miles south of Chicago, Illinois. The district's population estimate is 21,071, with 98.6 percent Caucasian, .5 percent Hispanic, .3 percent Asian, .2 percent other. Age groups are: 24 percent ages 0–17; 8.6 percent ages 18–24; 27.7 percent ages 25–44; 21.5 percent ages 45–64; 18 percent ages 65 and over. The per capita personal income is estimated at $17,480, with 10.5 percent below the poverty level.[1]

The city of Robinson is home to the RPLD's main location, and has a population of 7,200 people. Full literacy services are available at the

Robinson Public Library (RPL), with resource materials and tutoring space available at the three library branches in the towns of Oblong, Flat Rock, and Hutsonville. Further literacy outreach programs include Lawrence Public Library in Lawrence County and the Robinson Correctional Center in Robinson.

The RPLD is supported primarily by tax dollars. Additional grants fund special projects and some equipment updates. The library's Adult Literacy Partners Program is funded by annual acceptance of an Illinois Secretary of State Literacy Office grant. Private grant awards fund special projects and literacy initiatives. Governance structure includes a publicly elected Board of Trustees, with the library director and the literacy director both reporting directly to the board.

How Literacy Became Part of What We Do

In 1985, RPLD's special services librarian, Dena Wilson, responded to a grant opportunity from the Illinois State Library to initiate local adult literacy services within public libraries using community volunteers as tutors. Wilson explained: "At the time that we got the invitation to apply for a literacy grant, the library was already involved in several volunteer programs. We were using volunteers to help with reading for the blind, homebound delivery. . . . I simply looked at an adult reading program as another way to reach people who weren't already being served and to increase volunteerism. It made sense to me that literacy services would be offered at the library. As the reading level improves, a person can better utilize the *full* range of public library resources."

With this perspective guiding their actions, Wilson and Mary Crum, reading coordinators with the Robinson Community School District, went to an information meeting on how to submit a literacy grant proposal. The meeting was held by the Illinois Secretary of State's Literacy Office in Springfield.

Robinson's first literacy grant proposal was not approved. Funding, instead, was awarded to an area community college with a classroom instruction approach. "Although we were glad that our area of the state received funding, we were disappointed that the one-on-one tutoring aspect of our proposal did not receive approval. The one-on-one learning relationship seemed different and more appropriate for some adults." (Today, RPL's literacy program and area colleges use a referral system to actively share resources and information and to best serve adults based on learner needs, skills, and schedules.)

Determined to submit a 1986 grant proposal, Wilson sought a project director who was both well-qualified and free to devote full attention to launching the new service. Wilson and Crum shared the vision for a one-on-one adult literacy program with Dorothy Magill, a recently retired reading coordinator with the Palestine Community School District. "Dorothy took the project and ran with it," recalls Wilson.

Magill and Crum wrote a successful grant, and in 1986 the Adult Literacy Partners program was added to full-time RPLD services. That first year, Magill directed the program and was the only person on staff. "We ran an extensive recruitment campaign asking for community volunteers," explained Magill. "Our local newspaper, *Daily News,* donated thousands of dollars in free advertising to help us get the word out. As a result, 25 community volunteers were certified as reading tutors at the first tutor training series."

Curriculum and materials were purchased from Literacy Volunteers of America, Laubach, and other established literacy providers. Building the collection was a main objective the first year. "Almost all of the first year's grant funding went to buying materials for students to use," remembers Magill. Initial learner assessments and tutor matching were also done exclusively by Magill.

"Library support was exceptional," stated Magill. "We had marvelous cooperation from the library staff and library board. The first two years we didn't even have a phone, so they were constantly taking messages, running back and forth to help." Space for the literacy program was created out of a storage area and renovated to accommodate an office in a private tutoring area. "We all had to work together to make it work," remarked Magill.

The next year the Secretary of State's Literacy Office asked Magill to write a literacy grant to include Lawrence County. In 1987 Adult Literacy Partners (ALP) expanded to include services at the Lawrence Public Library in Lawrenceville, Illinois. An outreach coordinator for Lawrence County and an assistant for Crawford County were also included in the program's expansion. By the time Magill left the Literacy Program in August 1987, more than 100 students in both counties had been served. Over the next ten years, the ALP program continued to recruit and train community volunteers, recruit and serve adult learners, expand and improve curriculum and learners' assessment materials, network with other literacy providers at statewide conferences, and promote regular library use among adult learners.

In 1991 Robinson opened a medium-security Illinois State Correctional Center with 1,200 male inmates. The Illinois Secretary of State asked ALP to institute a Tutor Training Outreach program for inmates interested in becoming volunteer tutors for other inmates. Today, ALP reports an annual average of 50 inmates trained and certified as tutors, and a monthly average of 825 volunteer tutoring hours with inmate students.

Also in 1991, a monthly newspaper supplement called *Choices* began running in the *Daily News* and *Lawrence Daily Record*. Birthed under a Family Literacy grant, and designed to bring family and adult literacy issues into the homes of county residents, the local newspaper became cosponsor and sole funder of this project. Today, *Choices* is delivered free each month to more than 12,000 readers in a two-county area. The newspaper supplement features literacy and library services; local, national, and state literacy issues; and relates literacy with life while emphasizing rural culture and community interests.

In 1994 RPL welcomed a new director to literacy. Beth Hawkins brought a fresh perspective to the literacy program, realizing the changing needs for adults entering a technology-based workforce. "Although we were a viable program," explained Hawkins, "we were not progressing. A rural program needs to not lag behind the progress being made in urban areas. If we were going to produce people who were literate in all realms, not just in reading, we needed to experience a change in the program. We needed students involved in computer-assisted learning."

The LILAA Program

The ALP program received a surprise phone call in 1996 from the Lila Wallace-Reader's Digest Fund (LWRDF) out of New York. The Fund was soliciting grant applications from select programs in four states. Illinois was one of those states, and the Secretary of State's Literacy Office recommended Robinson. Hawkins remembers that new beginning: "The Fund called one day and I received a Federal Express package the next. They were eager to begin their library-literacy project called Literacy in Libraries Across America."

Hawkins's hope for the LWRDF grant was to help the literacy program organize, consolidate the curriculum, add computers and educational software designed for adults, and hire a special projects coordinator who would bring fresh ideas and new energy.

Funding in the amount of $150,000 was awarded to RPLD from the LWRDF in 1996. The focus of the three-year initiative was to improve existing library-based literacy programs by sharing best practices with the entire literacy field. Thirteen literacy programs in the U.S. were funded for the project. Robinson was the only rural site selected.

During the first two years of the Literacy in Libraries across America initiative, ALP retooled tutor training to make it more hands-on and interactive; offered computer learning including pre-GED, GED, phonics, and ESL software programs; instituted continuing education tutor work-shops to promote tutor retention (and thus affect student retention); hired a special projects coordinator to implement the objectives of the grant proposal; designed and generated student intake and tutor report forms; met with other public library literacy programs to learn and share; launched student and tutor recruitment efforts; and increased public awareness. "We were busy," recalls Hawkins.

Prior to the end of the LWRDF project, Hawkins resigned as literacy director, and special projects coordinator Konni Clayton assumed that position. "Since I was introduced to literacy through a project focusing on library-based programs, I just automatically emphasize the relationship between the library and the literacy program. We want literacy students to have a library card, use it, and explore other library services. We want our tutors to use library resources during learning sessions. A library is an ideal place to *not* know how to do something. Adult literacy students can feel at home in a library where others are there to learn something, too."

ALP submitted a grant proposal to the LWRDF in 1999 for another three-years' funding. Approved by the Fund, the current library literacy project focuses on learner retention. "What we are doing now," explained Clayton, "is examining the barriers adults have to learning, and then exploring ways we can implement strategies and services to address those needs. The Fund is looking for answers to 'How can we help adult learn-ers stay in a literacy program long enough to make meaningful differences in their lives?'" Clayton went on to say that the national average of length of stay in an adult literacy program is six months. "For adults who want to get a GED or learn English as a Second Language, six months is not that long," Clayton remarked, "especially when you consider that our volunteer tutors typically meet with their students once a week for about an hour each session."

The special LWRDF grant funding has allowed ALP to offer more services to adult learners than ever before: free child care, free transportation, extended evening and Saturday office hours, goal-setting assistance, additional computers and software, student orientation classes, and, most notably, the involvement of a student advocate on staff. The student advocate contacts every learner in the program on a regular basis to address barriers, communicate needs to the rest of the literacy staff, and encourage retention in the learning program. The student advocate also has instituted an incentive/reward system for adults as they continue to reach goals and make progress.

One step at a time, literacy at the Robinson Public Library has moved from vision to reality. Today, the program serves approximately 250 community learners with some 60 volunteer tutors, as well as more than 1,000 inmate students with 50 inmate tutors. Two full-time and three part-time members comprise the literacy staff.

The scope of the ALP program includes:

- Recruiting, assessing, retaining, and/or referring community and inmate adult students

- Recruiting, training, and retaining community and inmate volunteer tutors

- Targeting welfare-to-work clients, high school dropouts, non- or low-level readers, inmates at Robinson Correctional Center, "at-risk" high school students

- Increasing GED attainment rates by providing pre-GED and GED computer software/curricula

- Inviting English as a Second Language students to learn how to speak, read, and write English

- Creating computer learning/technology opportunities for low-literate adults

- Offering curriculum and other study materials appropriate and effective for adult learners

- Addressing and assessing learning style differences

- Maintaining a learner-centered program emphasis/direction

Continued

Furthering student involvement in lesson planning, goal setting, and student activities/newsletter

Partnering with other literacy providers, social service agents, and the Robinson Correctional Center to more fully/better serve shared clients and populations

Providing tutors with continuing education and tutoring techniques through tutor workshops and in-service training

Generating public support for a literate community

Collecting and maintaining accurate program information

Sharing best practices with local, state, and national literacy providers and libraries

Removing learning barriers to provide learners with educational, financial, social, cultural, and/or personal opportunities

Introducing and promoting the library as a lifelong learning resource

Service to adult learners includes:

Basic reading and writing assistance

Complete GED preparation

English as a Second Language instruction

Computer learning with pre-GED, GED, ESL, and other instructional software

Learning style assessment

Reading and math assessments

Referrals

Resume writing assistance and employment referrals (verifying tutoring instruction)

Family literacy and parenting information

Today, Dena Wilson, the special services librarian who first answered the call to include literacy as a Robinson Public Library service, is director of the Library District. She remains a strong advocate for literacy at the library. "Literacy services are not a deviation from library services," she explains. "Literacy, really, is part of library service responsibility. Literacy is in line with what we are already doing in public libraries."

> The stated mission of the Robinson Public Library is to provide materials and services for the educational, cultural, and recreational requirements of the community, recognizing diverse and special needs without discrimination. As a social institution, the Library also exists to bring people together both in groups and in understanding. The Library shall vigorously promote its function in the community, provide full access to a broad variety of materials and information, including beyond the local collection, and function with efficiency and courtesy to provide a pleasant environment. The Library shall welcome cooperation with other community organizations and institutions to further these goals.

Literacy Program director Clayton believes that "welcome cooperation" is the key element in the story of how a rural public library started a literacy program in Illinois. Clayton concluded: "When minds cooperate with motivation, visions are born. When actions cooperate with plans, goals take shape. When people welcome the process, success is inevitable!"

For more information about Adult Literacy Partners at the Robinson Public Library District in Robinson, Ill., write to: Adult Literacy Partners, Robinson Public Library, 606 N. Jefferson, Robinson, IL 62454, or call (618) 544-2917. Our e-mail address is robdlib@shawnet.shawls.lib.il.us.

Nina G.'s Story

Nina G. came to the Literacy Program at the Lawrence Public Library in 1991 with a fourth-grade reading level. Her story is one of persistence and dedication from both herself and her long-time tutor, Lois McKelfresh.

Nina completed the seventh grade in school but had problems with her short-term memory. It became her desire to obtain her GED, so she sought the help of Adult Literacy Partners, and was matched with a volunteer who made the decision to help Nina as best she could.

Nina and Lois worked steadily, preparing for the GED. They felt they had made enough progress that Nina could go and take the social studies portion of the test. Sadly, they never made it to testing day. Nina was suddenly diagnosed with cancer. She had to undergo surgery, chemotherapy, and other rehabilitation efforts. As a result, Nina's memory was affected even more. Medication and scarred emotions frustrated Nina and her tutor.

A staff note written in her file read: "We can not say when Nina will be ready to take the test. It would have been a real morale booster if she could have passed at least one. We do not have a solution to Nina's problem, but we hope that with continued good health she might recover some of her abilities."

Nina's tutor did not give up. She befriended Nina and encouraged her to keep trying. Nina worked very hard in pursuit of her educational goal. We are pleased to share that on July 14, 1999, Nina G. passed her GED and received her certificate! She told us: "My family didn't believe that I passed! I had to show them my certificate!" Nina is now using the computer in the Literacy Office, acquainting herself with the keyboard and software programs. Her goals are to take a basic computer class through the community college or the Senior Citizens Center. Whatever she decides to do, you can bet Nina will not give up.

Nina's is a story of possibilities—what might be with support, encouragement, direction, and persistence.

A Mexican Mother's Story

Piedad Bedoy, originally from Mexico, attended school in her native country through the ninth grade. After moving to Texas, she began taking GED classes, but moved to Lawrenceville, Ill., before she had earned her degree. Piedad learned of Adult Literacy Partners (ALP) through a Head Start coordinator after enrolling her children in Head Start classes. After initial intake and assessment, Piedad was matched with long-time volunteer tutor Joanna Buchanan. The tutoring partners set their long-range goals: to improve Piedad's English-language skills and to work on essay writing for the GED.

While working one-on-one with her ALP tutor, Piedad enrolled in a Frontier Community College GED Constitution class taught at the Lawrence Public Library by head librarian Linda Phillippe. Piedad took advantage of many literacy program opportunities, including adult learner computer and software programs such as GED Interactive and Berlitz English. She also worked with traditional texts and curricula to practice essay writing and language skills. As a result of her diligence and multilevel approach to learning, Piedad completed the Constitution class, took the GED test, and passed.

The impact that learning has had on Piedad has not stopped with her GED certification. She continues to be an advocate for learning within the literacy program, her community, and her family. Specifically, Piedad has been involved in:

- recruiting and encouraging other adult learners
- attending Literacy Task Force meetings to share the adult learner perspective on adult literacy issues
- demonstrating educational computer software at tutor continuing education workshops
- completing her first college-level course (computers)
- continuing college course instruction at Wabash Valley College, Mount Carmel, Ill.
- assisting other Spanish-speaking students
- working part-time at Head Start
- acting, most recently, as keynote speaker at Frontier Community College's GED graduation ceremony

The collaboration of several agencies, and the efforts of the Illinois Secretary of State's Literacy Office, have been significant in supporting Piedad's learning goals. Adult Literacy Partners is proud to be a part of her success. The Piedad Bedoy story reveals the power available when literacy and life connect!

The Story of a Cambodian Immigrant

Hong Tran, originally from Cambodia, came to the literacy program in October 1998. He needed to learn to speak, read, and write in English. Hong was born and raised in Vietnam, later moving to France and, lived there for 17 years. English will be his third language.

Hong began tutoring with Michele Nash on October 27, 1998, and they have become a perfect tutoring team. They have studied grammar/parts of speech, holidays/American culture, common medical terms/parts of the body, driving rules and road signs, and much more. Hong has made significant progress from his sessions by recently passing the written portion of the Illinois driver's test. Hong and Michele are currently working on banking services, such as credit applications, checking accounts, etc. Along with Michele's help, Hong also works independently on the student computer using the Learn to Speak English software.

Hong has a busy schedule, working six days a week with his brother at a very successful restaurant in Robinson. His most difficult task at work is mastering telephone skills. Hong makes his tutoring sessions a big priority. There is no doubt he will conquer telephone communication in the near future. Hong was selected as one of ten Illinois Spotlight on Achievement Award winners in 2000. He recently took a trip to Vietnam and Hong Kong and sent his tutor a postcard using complete sentences and proper spelling in English. It is obvious the library's literacy program has had a definite impact on Hong's life.

Randy R.'s Story

Randy R. became interested in the Adult Literacy Partners when he realized he could not read as well as his eight-year-old son. For many years Randy was able to tell his little boy stories by looking at the pictures in a book, but he could not read the words. As his son got older, Randy was unable to fool him into believing that Dad was really reading. This was Randy's motivation for becoming an adult learner.

When Randy came to us he had a resistive attitude, not really sure that he wanted our help. Even though he completed 11 years of school, Randy was only at a first-grade reading level. Randy has had a problem with drug and alcohol addiction for many years, which is another barrier to his learning.

With a little coaxing, we were able to match Randy with a tutor who was also new to the adult literacy program. These two men have become a devoted team. Randy values his tutor's help and is so happy with the progress they have made. Along with faithful tutoring sessions, Randy also studies phonics and spelling on the student computer. This computer work is a very big accomplishment for Randy. He was completely against using a computer at first, but with help and encouragement, he has become a regular computer user.

NOTE

1. *1998 Illinois Statistical Abstract*, Bureau of Economic and Business Research, College of Commerce and Business Administration, University of Illinois at Urbana-Champaign.

. 10 .

Theme-Based Instruction and Tutor Training at the New York Public Library Centers for Reading and Writing

DECKLAN FOX

The New York Public Library's Centers for Reading and Writing developed its theme-based curriculum within the subject areas of health and history. The history curriculum was conducted first, then the health curriculum was developed and administered. My focus in this chapter is the health curriculum. Three of the eight Centers for Reading and Writing sites participated in this educational project.

We started with a needs assessment to determine a list of topics within the health field that students would like to learn about. The result of the needs assessment was a list of diseases, which included asthma, heart ailments, diabetes, and hypertension. We decided by consensus that we would focus on prevention by doing a curriculum on wellness. We asked the question: "What is good health?" Students were asked to write about a time they needed more information about health. They were also asked to describe that time and what they did to get the information needed.

During this process, information was obtained from the Community Service Society of New York, an organization that is educating Medicaid recipients about the imminent conversion of their health coverage to managed care.

A Wellness Curriculum

Based on our need to present a health curriculum about wellness, we used the information garnered from the student surveys, student responses to the questions asked about their health-care experiences, and advice from our education and assessment consultants to create a six-session theme-based curriculum on health. The sessions met once per week for two hours.

The first session was a workshop on managed care, which was conducted by volunteers from the Community Service Society of New York. The second and third sessions focused on the questions "What is good health?" and "What is a healthy diet?" respectively. The fourth session covered "How to read and interpret nutritional labels." Exercise and its importance was next to follow, with stress management rounding out the curriculum. Before the sessions began, we conducted a survey developed by the Centers for Reading and Writing staff and our assessment consultant. Questions and information prompts included the following:

1. What is managed care?
2. Name an item found on a food label; and
3. On a scale from 1 to 5, with 5 being the highest,
   how would you rate the importance of exercise
   in your daily life?

These questions and prompts were given to students on the first day of the project. The same questionnaire was given to students at the conclusion of the curriculum as a means of assessing what was learned. The topics covered in the curriculum were included in the pre- and post-questionnaires.

During the development of the curriculum, materials were received from a variety of sources that included personnel from neighborhood hospitals, clinics, community-based organizations, and from students and volunteer tutors. Neighborhood presenters spoke on different topics such as diet, handling stress, and using the World Wide Web as a resource. For the sessions on nutritional labels, students brought in food packages and cans from home, and these labels became their reading material for that evening. Tutors and site staff were instrumental in assisting students with this process. Tutors conducted workshops and articulated connections between the theme and its application to students' daily lives. They brought in materials and demonstrated exercise and yoga techniques. Tutor involvement was evident in the presentation and planning of the curriculum. Advisory groups consisting of tutors and students were formed to help disseminate information to their peers. Tutors played an invaluable role in our past projects and are expected to continue in that vein in the future.

A student from one of the Centers wrote this piece on one of the topics covered, called "Reading Food Labels."

> I learned a lot about health. I never read the labels on the foods I brought before the health project at the Center, but now I am reading them. I learned about the foods that have vitamins such as vegetables and fruits. I learned that oranges give fiber to the diet and that animal products such as red meat, cheese, and milk have cholesterol. I also learned that drinking six glasses of water each day is good for my health and a good diet will keep me healthy.

This and other writings can be found on the New York Public Library Centers for Reading and Writing home page nypl.org/branch/literacy/. Student writings, journals, illustrations, photographs, and sound recordings will be included. Future technology plans supported by the Lila Wallace-Reader's Digest Literacy in Libraries Across America grant include the integration of computers, audio, and video into instruction. PCs are currently being used for e-mail, Internet, word processing, and other applications. As we continue to grow technologically, the focus on media literacy, which includes the use of video and television programs to improve literacy skills, will be enhanced accordingly. Each Center for Reading and Writing has at least six PCs and three video TVs, along with a variety of state-of-the-art audio equipment.

Tutor Training

The creation of a comprehensive tutor-training manual that captures the essence of the Centers for Reading and Writing's tutor-training curriculum is also a work in progress. This is a key element necessary to improve core program services. An updated tutor-training curriculum for preservice and in-service sessions, driven by centralized coordination and teams of trainers, is an element that is crucial to the successful development of a competent volunteer core. Training materials will cover small-group instruction, technology-assisted instruction mentored by volunteers, theme/goal-based instruction, and volunteer supported ESOL literacy programming. The manual will also include a sequence of pretraining activities to assist with the screening of prospective volunteers, and to inform them of the scope of the library's programming before participating in formal training.

Creating the Tutor-Training Manual

A consultant was hired to research and write the tutor-training manual. There are five phases to the process: Gathering, Synthesizing, Generating, Staff Development, and Implementation.

PHASE 1

Gather information regarding the current state of tutor-training workshops offered at the Centers for Reading and Writing

Site visits are made to present clarification of workshop goals and organization. Also, a needs assessment is conducted to elicit ways to improve current training and to provide ongoing tutor support in the form of in-services. All Centers for Reading and Writing sites submit curriculum materials.

PHASE 2

Synthesize information and collate materials gathered from each site

Site staff have an opportunity to view materials, prioritize topics, and select presentation order. Discussion during the meetings should result in an initial manual outline with topics sequenced to reflect general staff views.

PHASE 3

Generate the manual

During this phase, chapters will be submitted for review by Centers for Reading and Writing administrative staff as they are completed.

Material from Literacy Volunteers of America's *Tutor: A Collaborative Approach to Literacy Instruction,* seventh edition; *Litstart: Strategies for Adult Literacy and ESL Tutors,* third edition; and Queens Borough Public Library's *Literacy Tutor Training Manual* is incorporated along with other information provided by Centers for Reading and Writing sites.

PHASE 4
Staff development

Key Essentials:

- Helping to set a uniformed curriculum
- Activities that are included should match program objectives
- Determining tutor/tutor-training assessment that is relevant and easily administered
- Negotiating the role of cross-site participation in tutor training

PHASE 5
Implementation

- Scheduling orientations and tutor training at regular intervals
- Using the tutor-training manual in actual tutor-training sessions

To this end, the implementation phase is preceded by a coordinated outreach effort to radio stations and community newspapers to spread the word about planned orientations. By utilizing local media outlets, we seek interested volunteers to participate in orientations that may lead to successful tutoring experiences at one or more of our Centers.

Similar outreach is conducted to attract students to particular Centers that are in need. Orientation and tutor-training schedules are made available so that interested parties are aware of openings in their local libraries. The orientation, which consists of a presentation of a myriad of activities and services provided by the Centers, plus an introduction to our education philosophy, is an excellent way to initiate interested volunteers to the Centers for Reading and Writing. If sufficiently influenced by the orientation, prospective volunteers are advised to attend an interview with the site manager to state whether or not they have an interest in continuing the process by attending the 18- to 20-hour tutor-training sessions. The interview can also be used as a screening process to determine eligible candidates.

The New York Public Library's Centers for Reading and Writing view tutor training as an integral part of our service to the literacy community. Whether the focus is on theme-based, small-group, ESOL literacy, or technology instruction, or a combination of all of the above, a prepared tutor is a priceless resource.

Suggested Reading and Internet Resources

Adult Literacy Resource Institute: http://www2.wgbh.org/mbweis/ltc/alri.html

Apps, J. W. *Mastering the Teaching of Adults.* Malabar, Fla.: Krieger, 1991.

Blankenship Cheatham, J. *Tutor: A Collaborative Approach to Literacy Instruction.* Syracuse, N.Y.: Literacy Volunteers of America, 1993.

DuPrey, A. *Maintaining the Balance: A Guide to 50/50 Management.* Syracuse, N.Y.: Literacy Volunteers of America, 1992.

Freire, P. *Pedagogy of Hope.* New York: Continuum, 1992.

_____. *Pedagogy of the Oppressed.* New York: Continuum, 1970.

Frey, P. *Litstart: Strategies for Adult Literacy and ESL Tutors.* Okemos, Mich.: Michigan Literacy, 1999.

Literacy Assistance Center: http://www.lacnyc.org

Mayher, J. S. *Uncommon Sense.* Portsmouth, N.H.: Boynton/Cook, 1990.

The New York Public Library:
   http://www.nypl.org/branch; nypl.org/branch/literacy/

. 11 .

No Simple Answers

BRUCE CARMEL and ANITA CITRON

At the Queens Borough Public Library's Adult Literacy Programs, we long for simple answers. How many students do we serve? What kind of services do we offer? Are we a library or a literacy program? Even the name of the place where we work requires an explanation. "The Queens Borough Public Library?" "Where is that?" In New York City, in the Borough of Queens. New York City has three library systems. We are one of them. New Yorkers don't know that (it comes from the time when Brooklyn and Queens were not part of New York City), and hardly anyone in the rest of the library/literacy world does either.

Literacy Programs and Libraries

Are we a literacy program or a library? We are both, as most library literacy programs are. That often requires explanations. We are part of the library, but the nature of the service we provide is different from many other programs in the library. The level of service we provide is often more intimate and intensive than the service provided to the average library user. We are a full-fledged literacy program, but being part of the library gives us access to certain other resources that other literacy programs don't have. We have easier access to the many resources, programs, and services that the library provides. Class visits and deposit collections are a big part of what we do.

Libraries are about access and so are literacy programs. Balancing access and need is a challenge. We are open to everyone, but we have limited resources. The resources must be distributed. There are not enough computers. There is not enough space. There are not enough tutors. There are not enough spaces in classes. Also, issues of privacy and confidentiality surface. Adult beginning readers don't want their friends and neighbors pointing at them through the library windows. But we are a library and open to everyone.

What kind of services do we offer? There is a range. Some students study with us for hours every day. They use the computers. They listen to tapes. They work with tutors in small groups. They attend classes. They take videos, books, and audiotapes home to study. Other students check out something from the collection and we never see them again. Most students are something in between.

We like that flexibility. Many of our students work. Many have family responsibilities. Some people's schedules change with the seasons or from day to day: the kids are on summer vacation, work is real busy now and I can pick up some overtime, they moved me off the graveyard shift. We want to be able to fit into people's lives, so we have to be flexible.

Our Students

How many students do we serve? It depends on what we count. We have gate counts. We also have counts of students who go through an orientation, get pretested, get matched with a tutor, and take a post-test a few months later. They are very different numbers. About 7,000 students "use" our programs. English-for-Speakers-of-Other-Languages (ESOL) classes enroll about 3,000 each year. ESOL tutoring enrolls about 1,000 each year. Basic Education tutoring enrolls about 500 students each year. The others use computers and other forms of guided self-study.

Those were some relatively simple questions and some relatively complicated answers. And those were the easy questions. Now for the hard one: How do we teach adults how to read, write, and speak English?

To the uninitiated, the provision of literacy instruction should seem, on the face of it, a cut-and-dried activity: Train the tutors, find the students, match them up and test every 50 hours. As was once stated (somewhat infamously) at a meeting of New York City literacy practitioners, "Get 'em in, get 'em literate, and get 'em out." And yes, from a distance, that is what it is. But step in a little closer and the picture that comes into focus is a complicated, multifaceted scenario that abounds with many subplots, twists, and turns.

How We Teach

First of all, reading, writing, and speaking English are complex. One skill that is important is *analyzing*. That means reading and listening critically. Not dead decoding, not mechanical sounding out, but engaging with a text and with speech, applying knowledge, approaching print and speech as meaningful. Analysis on a basic level involves questions like "What does this mean?" as well as "Who wrote this and what are they trying to get me to believe, to do, or to buy?"

The goals of our students are varied but commonly expressed as wanting to "learn how to read and write" or "learn to speak English." To many of our students, a good student is passive and receptive. This idea comes from experience. It's as if they are saying, "I am gonna swallow this nasty, nasty medicine [an education] no matter how bad it tastes." With basic education (BE) students, it is altogether possible that we are dealing with adults who have never approached print with anything less than trepidation and hesitation. Perhaps they have never had stories read to them or even discussed one after having read it. Print to them is a source of misery. You cannot expect pleasure in reading in people who experience it as *anything but* pleasure. For this you must develop a sense of what "reading" really is. You have to experience reading with a purpose other than "reading to improve your reading."

Tutors deliver much of our instruction. They are deeply committed and they do a great job. We train our tutors in what we feel is progressive and sound methodology. We encourage tutors to find out what the students are interested in, what they want to learn how to do, what literacy tasks they face day to day. But our students often want very traditional teacher-centered instruction. ("You're the teacher so teach me.") A tutor or a teacher who asks, "What do you think we should start with today?" may be seen as unprepared by a student with traditional ideas about the role of the teacher. Where do we go from there?

Collaboration can only occur when there are two or more parties willing to take part in the process. We have to negotiate. If a student wants to start by memorizing the dictionary, we can't say, "I hear what you are saying, but I am not going to teach you that way." We are more likely to find other ways to use a dictionary, talk about why we want to use a different approach, and get into activities right away so the student can get some satisfaction.

This is a great challenge for us, and perhaps *the* great challenge of adult education: How do we negotiate what we know about good reading, writing, and language-learning with the students' and tutors' ideas of what school should be?

Reflection and innovation are expensive in terms of time when you are trying to deliver services when you are continually improving them. But there is no other way. Luckily, our Adult Learning Center's professional staff is full-time. We have time to meet, to read articles, to look at websites. Still, none of us have the luxury (or the desire) to stop providing services while we redesign what we do. So we try out new things as the program keeps chugging along, doing our best to assess the impact of innovations.

We have always seen the training and support of tutors as having great potential as a leverage point. This year we took a deep breath, pulled back the camera lens, and took a good look at the situation. Our tutors are dedicated, generous, intelligent people who want to help others. We decided we needed to support them better. We decided we needed to be clearer with the volunteers about what they were supposed to be doing. We decided to move away from an intensive up-front training that tried to cover everything you always wanted to know about adult education but were afraid to ask, and give tutors a strong and simple foundation on which to build.

For ESOL tutors, our training now focuses on facilitating a conversation group. They learn how to get a conversation going, how to encourage students to talk to each other, how to model usage, and how to deal with correction. Grammar instruction, the Internet, reading the newspaper, games, writing exercises, and a whole lot more come later or someplace else. For literacy tutors, we have offered a more focused training on facilitating reading clubs. They learn how to facilitate book selection, discussions, and predictions. They learn how to move students from being read to to reading with a tutor to reading on their own. They learn about choral reading, shadow reading, and silent reading.

Aside from the plasticity of the idea, we are hoping that with this as the students' first introduction to reading instruction, they will adjust their attitudes towards learning as this method will disabuse them of the passivity that marked their former experience. The reading clubs actively encourage approaching reading on a truly whole-language approach.

This is a way to introduce tutors to reading on a level that avoids the specific and heads to the general, which, in this case, is learning how to "read." Not using the small skills, but guessing the word from context, from prediction, from learning to follow the idea of a story. It is, in truth, having students combine a skill they already have, i.e., verbal expression, with print material. The book, we hope, will no longer be seen as involving specific skills they don't have and that require drill and practice, but rather as an extension of their lives and within their abilities.

These are the foundation on which we can build. We are a whole-language program. We believe that reading, writing, speaking, and listening are connected. We believe that skills can be taught in the context of meaning. But we don't think volunteers can do all of that right away, not even after the fairly intensive perservice training we used to offer.

Support for Tutors and Students

We also decided we needed to build in more mechanisms for ongoing support. Monthly tutor meetings (that only some people attend) and a yearly conference (that only some people attend) were worthwhile but not enough. Ongoing support was not built in. We had to catch tutors on the way out, the way in, or during their stay. For some new trainings we have developed, tutors are told that the volunteer commitment involves tutoring and meeting with staff on a regular basis. After each session of our Summer Reading Clubs, the tutor will meet with a professional staff member to discuss the day's activity. This is a great opportunity to keep the tutor focused on reading and understanding that the acquisition of this skill is more dependent on the verbalizing than on decoding. Tutors so far have welcomed the chance to get support, advice, and time to talk about what is going on with the group.

There are other areas where we want to continue to grow and change. We already provide orientation for students, but we want to refine that, helping students get a better handle on what to expect from our program and what we expect from them. Goal setting is something else we want to refine. Students are telling us that they want a better understanding of the connection between their long-term goals and dreams and what they do at the centers day to day.

We try to focus on the purpose of the program. What are we trying to accomplish? What should students who leave our program be able to do? What do the students want to achieve and how can we use the resources we have (such as volunteers) to help them achieve that? There are no simple answers to these questions. We just need to keep reminding ourselves of that.

12

Creating a Community of Readers to Fight Functional Illiteracy

STEVE SUMERFORD

Every morning when I was a child, my grandparents would get up an hour early so they would have time to read the morning paper and some selections from the Bible before they headed off to work at the textile mill. At the time, it never occurred to me that my grandparents had limited literacy skills. It was only when I was a teenager that I realized that it took them many hours every week to read their five-page Sunday-school lesson.

My grandmother told me in the last year of her life, that due to her poor reading skills she had read only one book from cover to cover in the last 30 years. She also told me that she had never been in a public library.

If my grandparents were entering the workforce today with this same level of skills, they would certainly be relegated to low-paying jobs. Even the kinds of assembly-line jobs that they had in the textile mills are almost gone now, replaced by those that require more advanced reading, critical thinking, and computer skills. My grandparents would be among the ranks of the 40 million Americans today who lack functional literacy skills. Perhaps they would also be searching for a literacy program, and I hope they would call their local public library for help. I also hope their library would have a program for them and all of the others in their town who wanted to learn to read and write.

In 1996, when the folks at the Lila Wallace-Reader's Digest Fund decided to grant $4 million to support model literacy programs in public libraries, they were expressing their faith in libraries and providing librarians with an

A version of this article appeared in *American Libraries*, May 1997.

opportunity to reclaim literacy as an issue that is at the very heart and soul of our institutions.

A national spotlight is shining on the illiteracy problem. Former-President Clinton, the nation's governors, leading educators, and business leaders are all talking about the need for more effective literacy programs. Recent economic and demographic trends have also reawakened our nation's awareness that functional illiteracy is a growing problem. The advent of welfare reform, the growing number of immigrants who do not speak English, and the demand for a different type of workforce are also highlighting the need for more effective adult literacy programs.

Libraries are at a critical juncture. They have the opportunity to become a key component of the new literacy initiatives. While the decision about whether to provide only minimal services, such as an adult learning collection, or to offer full-scale literacy instruction programs should be based on the specific needs of each local community, we would be remiss if we ignored the national calls from the president on down for expanded literacy efforts.

It may be difficult to contemplate adding a new literacy effort to our already very full plates, especially since technology is absorbing more and more of our resources. However, literacy work in the Information Age looks very different from the phonics-based curriculum of a decade ago. If we view literacy programs from this new framework, we may see that they are a natural part of our basic work, rather than a diversion from what seems to be our technology-driven services.

Rather than seeing technology and literacy as competing budgetary and personnel demands, we have a unique opportunity to not only make our technological resources and expertise available to literacy providers and students but to demonstrate to the nation the powerful role we can play in addressing one of the nation's most critical problems.

To move away from a commitment to adult literacy at this time could be a very serious strategic mistake for libraries. The nation is looking to us to help solve this crisis. Almost every speech or article written about illiteracy mentions libraries as one of the key institutions in the literacy campaign.

Literacy as the Library's Mission

In 1989, as assistant director of Greensboro Public Library here in North Carolina, Sandy Neerman led an effort to make promotion of literacy a core component of the library's mission. Rather than seeing literacy as an optional service or a project you do only when grant funding is available, Neerman wanted a commitment to literacy to be as closely identified with the library as are reference services, recreational reading, and children's programs.

"When literacy is understood as a part of your core mission, you approach it very differently. You don't just create a department or a special project. When literacy is a part of your mission, it is woven into everything you do," Neerman said.

Now as director of Greensboro, Neerman believes that "with every major decision librarians make, we have to ask ourselves how it impacts our community's illiteracy problem." When the Greensboro Library staff is designing a new building or renovating an old one, we try to create tutoring rooms and learning centers. When we allocate the book budget, we take money for literacy books and software right off the top. When we hire staff, no matter where they will be working, we try to be sure that they are sensitive to and supportive of literacy efforts.

Rather than automatically launching a new tutorial program, Neerman and the other staff sought input from grassroots community leaders. These leaders consistently pointed out the gaps in the city's existing literacy programs. What became clear to the library staff was the need for new literacy services and programs, and an even greater need for strategic planning and the creation of an infrastructure to develop appropriate literacy services and to advocate for literacy students.

As reported previously, three in four direct-provider libraries (78.1%) collaborate with an outside agency or program to provide adult literacy tutoring or instruction. *Survey*, p. 24

Libraries most often provide classroom space and instructional materials, while the partnering organizations most often supply literacy instructors and publicity—and, particularly, recruit learner. Partnerships are most often based on an "informal/verbal agreement" (67.6%) rather than on a legal or binding contract. *Survey*, p. 26

Of those libraries that are not direct providers, most (73.1%) reported being in communities where other agencies already provide literacy tutoring and instruction. *Survey*, p. 5

With this knowledge, the staff and the Friends of the Library recruited representatives from ten key organizations, including the community college, an after-school tutoring program, a community-based adult literacy organization, and the public schools. With the understanding that a holistic, community-based approach would be most effective, they also recruited organizations that are not traditionally members of a literacy organization, such as the Health Department, the Junior League, a marketing firm, the Unemployment Office, a mental health association, and the Public Housing Authority. In honor of this community approach, rather than a single-agency approach, to literacy, the group decided to name the new network the Community of Readers.

Eight years later, the Community of Readers still meets every month at the Vance Chavis Library, one of Greensboro's oldest branches. Now the network includes more than 50 organizations. Each month the members share their successes, learn from each other, and work together to solve problems. The network has spawned several collaborative family literacy programs and reading-promotion campaigns.

According to June Swanston-Valdes, director of the Black Child Development Institute, one of the charter members of the network, the Community of Readers has been a great asset for her organization. "Where else can you go every month and find everyone from the health department to the local universities all talking about reading and literacy?"

When Neerman reflects on the success of the Community of Readers, she notes that this community-based approach to literacy has been the single most effective strategy for demonstrating to the city that librarians can be leaders, problem solvers, and community builders. "Our leadership in this area has led to a revitalization of the Friends of the Library, new funding for programs, and greater political clout. We have gained new lifelong library users and supporters. While helping hundreds of families improve their reading skills, we have also helped ourselves."

Literacy as a Family Value

People often wonder why the nation is not solving the illiteracy problem faster. The answer is that illiteracy is often the result of growing up without good literacy models in the home, and there are simply not enough effective programs to assure that parents are able to improve their own literacy skills. Because nonreading parents tend to raise nonreading children, educators have concluded that family-based literacy programs are an effective way to break this self-perpetuating cycle of illiteracy. Such family literacy programs teach basic reading skills to parents using a family-oriented reading curriculum. Children's librarians are uniquely qualified to develop and lead such family literacy programs. The Glenwood Library has developed a Family Learning Program in partnership with a local elementary school in a low-income neighborhood. The library staff trained volunteers from the Junior League who come to the library every week to provide literacy activities for parents and their children.

Another family literacy model is the Motheread project sponsored by the Chavis Library in partnership with an anti-poverty organization called Uplift. Children's librarian Bea Shaw goes to the public-housing community center every week, where several families come to learn reading techniques. In this project, the adult learners are empowered to make the decisions about the curriculum and the organization of the program. This learner-centered, participatory approach is based on a respect for the learners' culture and expertise.

Lou Sua (see chapter 13), librarian at the Chavis Library, discovered the learner-centered literacy work can empower adult students to move out of the shadows and into leadership roles in their communities. Sua coordinated a program called Parents Learning Together for women living in public housing.

"Many of these women didn't believe that they could read and write very well," Sua said. "We used a very nontraditional curriculum including newspapers, magazines, cookbooks, soap operas, and computers as our instructional materials. We used the entire library." Sua added that after a few months, most of the women had achieved a new level of confidence in their literacy skills and, consequently, many of them made some major changes in their lives.

Add Technology to the Mix

Lena Gonzalez, who coordinates English as a Second Language (ESL) classes for immigrants at the Glenwood Library, has found that computers can be effective teaching tools.

In addition to commercial ESL software programs, she finds that a simple word processor is valuable for whole-language reading and writing

> Learners in both types of literacy programs (ABE and ESL) are required or encouraged to use computers.
>
> Computer-assisted instruction (to improve/facilitate the process of literacy learning) was reported in 70.8% of ABE and 61.8% of ESL programs. *Survey,* p. 19

activities. "Computers allow students to easily type or dictate their own stories. Then these student-produced writings become part of the class curriculum." For more advanced learners, Gonzalez and students developed a special class that taught them how to write and produce a newsletter.

An ESL teacher for several years before she became a librarian, Gonzalez says that "the ability to click the mouse and leap to a homepage about your home country is very meaningful to a refugee or immigrant who is feeling homesick or a student who wants to show others in the class what his or her home country is really like."

Advanced ESL students are now working to create their own home-pages on the Web. Each group of students makes its own decisions about how the native country should be represented. Gonzalez observes that "since every student's homepage will have an e-mail option, I assume that the students will get lots of practice reading and writing in English."

As the nation moves into the Information Age, we cannot afford to leave anyone behind. Yet, according to some estimates, existing literacy programs reach only about 10 percent of the 40 to 50 million adults who need them. Libraries can be at the forefront of the effort to stem this growing crisis.

Librarians have to make sure that the very same resources we provide to the literate consumer are also available for those whose literacy is emerging. That means our technology, collections, facilities, and staff must support literacy. It means that each library's program could look very different from the others but that all of them are based on the needs and goals of the learners themselves.

If we involve literacy students in planning and evaluating our pro-grams, we will not only be assured of better programs but will also be building a deep and long-lasting sense of community with these men and women. This is ultimately the best way to break the cycle of illiteracy and create a true community of learners.

The Future

In 1999 we decided that the Community of Readers needed to be more than just an opportunity for networking and collaborating. We decided that without a strategic plan for literacy we would probably never succeed in raising the literacy levels for our community. A strategic plan would provide us with a blueprint that the entire city could use as a guide in decisions related to funding, programming, organizational development, and staff training.

To develop this strategic plan we decided that we needed input from two levels of the community. First, we wanted to hear from the grassroots—the learners, parents, teachers, and nonprofit leaders. Second, we needed the input and endorsement from the city's "movers and shakers." So we created a new project called Literacy 2000. We asked several of the city's leaders (college presidents, school superintendents, newspaper publishers, etc.) for their thoughts. To obtain the grassroots perspective, we held ten "listening sessions," where anyone could come to a session at the library and give us their thoughts on creating a more literate community.

Finally, in July 2000 we took all of this input and created a "Strategic Plan for Literacy in Greensboro." This 25-page document has been endorsed by numerous leaders and community groups. Based on the strengths, weaknesses, and opportunities that we found during the process of developing the plan, this document provides us with the goals, objectives, and action steps that will lead to a more literate community. Eight different action groups have been formed to implement the strategic plan.

Led by the staff of the public library and by dozens of community volunteers, the Community of Readers has now matured from a small network of committed teachers, tutors, and librarians to a community institution that has the potential to lead the city in creating new ways to deliver literacy services.

Our vision is that by 2005, there will be community-based learning centers where both children and adults can learn using a learner-centered curriculum. These centers will be filled with technology and volunteer tutors, but the vitality of the centers will derive from the fact that they will be managed by learners and neighborhood leaders. These centers will not be owned by any one institution but will be funded and supported by all of the literacy providers. These centers will be in schools, libraries, Head Start centers, neighborhood resource centers, churches, and small businesses.

Such centers will allow families to learn in their own neighborhoods at times that best meet their needs. This community-based approach to literacy will not only lead to a more literate citizenry but will also give learners and grassroots organizers a greater sense of empowerment. It will be a catalyst for increased civic participation to serve on the steering committee.

Greensboro Learners

My name is Graciela Kellar. I am from Panama and I have been living in North Carolina for four years. I decided to go to the library here because it is perfect place to learn. One of the reasons is the wonderful teachers that encourage their learners to do their best and show them also that they trust in them. Being a learner or a tutor is one of the most beautiful experiences for both sides. Each of them has a lot to share and they establish a common interest by sharing their own point of view about the life they used to have in their native country and also the life they are experiencing in this country. After they break the ice, different interesting topics come along. I believe this is one very strong way to learn by speaking and explaining your beliefs, values, and knowledge to someone else that you respect and trust.

Since I started offering my service in this institution as an AmeriCorps member, I have had the opportunity to meet new people and travel with them through experiences they share to their native countries. Besides that I can establish very close friendships with them and that makes me feel very happy. In this place I have learned to be more humble with the people around me.

This institution contains an umbrella of different programs at different hours that help learners have more access to the programs they wish to enroll in. It is a little bit hard to explain what I had been learning from my teachers because each of them has their own way of teaching, so at the end you learn more than what do you expect to learn. My life has been changed for good because I didn't speak English before I came here and now even though I am still working to improve it, I feel more comfortable with myself.

On the other hand, I hope that other institutions use this library as a model and bring programs that will help future learners to learn the language in similar places, probably in the future more and are more people are not going to feel the struggle as I felt one day. I encourage all the people to stop one day at the Glenwood Library and ask for all the different programs. Each of these programs is free and available for anyone who wants to learn and explore the programs. The librarians will be glad to assist you in all you need.

My name is Serigne Bachir Dieng. I am from Senegal, West Africa. I have been in the USA for almost twenty months. When I came to Greensboro, North Carolina, in April of 1999, I was not able to understand any of the language. Due to my foreign accent, my pronunciation makes my communication with people difficult. I found at that time that I had to go to school to improve my English. I chose the Glenwood library because it is a nice place to study and to make friends. I am a part of this library's literacy program as a learner and also an AmeriCorps member. Any progress I have made in comprehension and conversation can be attributed to the support I have received from the library's literacy program. I have learned many things; such as the basic computer skills in the computer English learning lab. I have also learned about people around the world during the weekly conversation club. The Glenwood library is my second home. It is a perfect place where immigrants and native-born Americans can get together in different activities. The staff of the Glenwood library has been most helpful in fostering the development of my job skills. They have been supportive in my effort to understand my job. Their encouragement has been most meaningful.

One of the valuable things I really like about the library's literacy program is you can have fun while you are learning. The ESL conversation club is a multicultural meeting where you can eat and laugh with people. In addition to providing people with very helpful reading materials, the Glenwood library gathers learners in a family where mutual respect reigns.

.13.

Serving This Community

LOU SAUNDERS SUA

It is very interesting that I have been asked to write a chapter in this publication. I would think that because I don't consider myself a traditional librarian or literacy provider that people would want to hear from someone who views librarianship or literacy in a more traditional role.

Librarianship and literacy were not fields of work that I planned for myself but where I feel that I was led through a plan from God. When I was in library school, the "nonusers" (patrons, customers, etc.) of the library, not the "users," always concerned me. I always figured that the "users" would get the services they needed from the library but that the "nonusers" would have to find something of value to really bring them to the library. I feel that what were considered "nonusers" of the library back in the 1980s are the people we are now seeing as adult learners and literacy students. While everyone was planning services and programs to meet the needs of the people who were already using the library, I was trying to figure out how to plan programs and services that could be taken to people who were not traditional users but who could become users.

Expanding Horizons

I came to work at the Greensboro Public Library as a children's librarian in the Southeast Branch (later changed to V. H. Chavis Lifelong Learning Branch Library). I was directly out of library school but at the time had 11 years of experience working in public and academic libraries. The first year on the job was challenging because I had not been involved in public libraries or work with children for five years. Those five years were spent working in academic libraries. After a year of children's work, I was given the opportunity to expand my career and work with teens. This was very challenging because it presented me with the chance to expand my skills and abilities. I was able to incorporate the skills that I had learned while working with the growing number of teens who were coming into my branch library. I also had a child who was approaching that age and I was looking for ways of managing the changes in him. We started presenting a series of workshops that we felt addressed the educational and informational needs of this age group. A series of workshops geared to high school students (grades 10–12) called "Soar to the T.O.P." was held to address the study skill needs of this age group. T.O.P. was the acronym for Teenage Opportunity Programs. Programs were planned and presented that not only included study skills but also job hunting, college prep, prom preparation, and car repair. While doing these programs, we were encountering teens who had babies and had issues that needed to be addressed.

The Greensboro Public Library system was also moving into a new area of work. We were beginning to do more with families in the area of family literacy. We started off with a pilot program titled "Catch 'em in the Cradle." This program consisted of a series of eight workshops that were held in public-housing communities. These workshops worked to encourage parents of young children up to five years of age to read to their children to help develop language skills and thereby develop reading skills. I volunteered to do four of these workshops and eventually became the coordinator of the program. When I went out into the community, I discovered that there were a number of issues involved in working with the families that I did not realize existed. Parents were concerned about their children's educational needs. But the more pressing needs of the family— such basics as food, shelter, and clothing—interfered with parents addressing these educational needs. We developed a number of programs to take to the community that addressed these needs and began to look at how to address some of the other needs of the community.

New Programs

Resulting from the family literacy work were programs that helped address some of the educational needs of the parents. Programs such as Parents Learning Together, Parents as Partners, and H.O.P.E (Helping Other People (and ourselves) to Be Empowered), helped to address the empowerment needs of the parents. When parents started feeling empowered in their homes, their communities, and their children's schools, they were more capable of addressing the educational needs of their children.

The library as an alternative to the community college offered parenting classes, GED classes, and computer instruction. People seemed to be more comfortable attending an off-site location to get some of their educational needs met. These programs addressed the needs of women from low-resource communities, who did not have the educational skills and resources to get beyond welfare. I use the term "low-resource" instead of low-income because you find that money is not the only resource that is lacking in homes and communities. I worked with the participants in the now defunct JOBS program through the Department of Social Services. This training included computer skills, parenting skills, community empowerment, and leadership skills. The family literacy programs continued in the community, but a number of these were directed more to teen moms involved in various other programs also in the community.

Always Facilitating

My work has been in serving as a facilitator of learning for the people in the community who wanted to get involved. This community in which I have worked for the last 12 years has proven to be the place that I had concerns about when I was in library school. I see my work in librarianship as a way of combining what I know and have learned with what I feel into the work that benefits the community and the library. I have listened for years to people who say that it is not the job of the library to serve as a teaching facility for the community. The public schools, community colleges, and other institutions are to serve those educational needs of the community. I see libraries as being the place for all learning to take place. I see it as our responsibility to provide for the community a safe environment to learn. I see that by helping to facilitate the learning of people in the community, we (librarians and literacy providers) are creating a new group of library advocates and customers. We should grasp the opportunities that are there for us and make a difference. Libraries and literacy go hand-in-hand.

Although this is not a community that I grew up in, this community looks like one I could have grown up in. There are so many needs to be met. There are people who are going to take advantage of what the library has to offer and there are people who won't. But I feel it is our responsibility to have those opportunities there when anyone decides it is their time. All people will never be at the same place at the same time, but they need to know that when their time comes that we, the community library, will be there to support them in their decisions. I look at the number of people I have worked with in the past 12 years and I see a lot of diversity in achievement. Some people have gone on to get a college education, some are working in jobs that they thought they never would have, some have gotten off public assistance and become homeowners, and some are in the same place they were in when they were involved in the programs. Those who have not achieved may or may not achieve but that is their choice. All of this is encouraging to me and makes me want to continue to work harder and to provide what is needed for the community.

I view literacy and people achieving their goals as a stepping-stone to the improvement of their lives, their children's lives, and the community. I have observed for those people who have not worked long-term in the community that when programs and services do not produce a great number of successes, they are ready to say that something didn't work. They are ready to pack up and move onto something that they feel will be successful. But what they feel is successful (or not) may not be how the community views success. I have always been an advocate of the community determining what's needed and what is successful. I have watched programs come and go in this community but the one thing that the community can count on is the library. We have been here and will be here when they are ready to move forward. We value their opinions both constructive and otherwise. This is how we know if we are meeting the needs of the community and doing a good job.

We get to know the children first. Then we usually get to know the parents through programming and other events that bring them together as a family. Once we get the family into the library, then the parents can see that the library is a nonthreatening place. When they realize that we can offer services and programs to help them move forward in their lives, we can make progress in meeting their needs and helping them achieve their goals.

I don't think there can be any other place for me than where I am right now. This work is very fulfilling because it allows me to see what a little change can do in someone's life. There is a commercial that touts "Change Is Bad." I don't view change that way. I think that when change is channeled in a positive direction with positive results then change is good. When we as librarians and literacy providers step up to the plate and show how we can help exact change in a community and people's lives, then I feel that God is pleased and makes it easier and more rewarding for us to carry on this much-needed work.

· 14 ·

Teaching Adult Literacy in a Multicultural Environment

GARY E. STRONG

I can't remember a time when I could not read. It seems as if it is something that I have always known how to do. My great-grandmother used to gather us up into her lap and tell us stories. She instilled in me the love of a good story and pushed me to read. It is hard to imagine someone whose life is devoid of something that is second nature to most of us.

But I have heard a grandmother speak tearfully about how difficult and shame-filled her life had been until she finally came to one of Queens Library's Adult Learning Centers to learn to read. And I have heard people who were considered well educated in the countries of their birth speak of their humiliation for having to struggle with the simplest of errands because they don't know English. I have known adults who were laid off from their jobs who couldn't read the want ads or complete a resume to apply for a new job. People who cannot read often feel unconnected and alone.

As one adult literacy student put it in writing for the student journal, "When I was a little girl I didn't get to go to school regularly like other children. I had to stay home and babysit while my mother and father went to work but I had a dream of going to school. I was 49 when I went back to school. One thing I know I can spell my name properly by the time I was twelve. I was a good cook and also washing and cleaning for my family. I never got to play with other children. I was too busy taking care of my sister and brothers. I gave up thinking about going back to school. There was no rainbow for me to hold onto."

The People's University

I have always believed in the public library as "the people's university." The public library, with its nonjudgmental mission, is a tremendous source of support and encouragement. Public libraries are guardians, not only of collections of books but of the right to read.

At Queens Library we believe that reading and writing are essential to maintaining a free and democratic society. Adults in Queens, regardless of native language, should have access to literacy instruction at the library. This includes:

- small-group instruction for adult new readers by trained volunteer tutors;
- conversation groups for adults learning English as an additional language;
- computer-assisted instruction for students learning English or improving their reading skills, which also facilitates basic computer literacy;
- adult basic education classes;
- collections of materials, including books, cassettes, and videotapes for adult new readers and those whose native language is not English; tutor-training workshops for adult literacy and English for Speakers of Other Languages conversation volunteers; and
- professional educators available for assistance and advisement.

Because Queens is one of the most ethnically diverse counties in the United States, our two million customers comprise almost every cultural and social background on the globe. Almost half speak languages other than English at home. Some never attended school as children. Still others, for any number of reasons, just never learned.

Queens Library offers several options for customers to obtain basic literacy skills. Formal classes in English for Speakers of Other Languages (ESOL) are offered in the spring and fall terms. Each term consists of 100 instructional hours and is taught by a certified ESOL teacher. Typically, some 3,000 students are enrolled, representing 85+ countries and speaking more than 45 different languages. Classes are held at the basic and intermediate levels. They may be held at library branches or in our Adult Learning Centers. There are even classes for ESOL students who are illiterate in their own languages. Amazingly, the drive to learn is so great, more than half of those students will go from not even knowing how to hold a pencil to basic English literacy classes in less than a year. Space and budget limit the number of students we can accommodate. The classes are in high demand: we turn away as many applicants as we can register. A lottery is held to select learners fairly.

Data from the survey also suggest that the demand for library-based literacy services exceeds the current supply. Waiting lists for ESL tend to be longer: 23.3% of ESL have "more than 50" persons, compared with only 10.6% for ABE. For ABE, the median waiting list is 15.0 persons; for ESL it is 21.0. *Survey*, p. 21

Queens Library's six Adult Learning Centers are within or adjacent to a regular library location and offer basic literacy and informal English conversation groups. Professional staff rely heavily on volunteer tutors to work with students one-on-one or in small groups. Teaching materials are geared toward adult interests and sometimes concentrate on specialized vocabulary, such as that needed to pass the test to get a driver's license, to negotiate public transportation, or, for more advanced students, to obtain a high school equivalency diploma. One student at our annual luncheon spoke proudly and tearfully about having just purchased her own home. While she had previously been able to afford it financially, she had never been able to negotiate the paperwork necessary to obtain the mortgage until she came to the Adult Learning Centers. On another occasion, I watched while a volunteer tutor worked patiently with a young man who had come to the Adult Learning Center because he wanted to get a job as a long-distance truck driver, but he couldn't read a map. Working with two sets of road atlases, the tutor proposed trips ("how would you travel from Akron, Ohio, to Miami, Florida?"), and the student worked out and verbalized the directions.

Cultural Sensitivity

Sensitivity to cultural differences is axiomatic to a successful learning experience. Our tutors are counseled not to make physical contact, however casual, with learners. They must be careful about using humor, as it often doesn't translate well. Asians hold teachers in the highest regard, and they may feel it is disrespectful to have the casual give-and-take conversations we rely on as learning tools. Hispanics often find it disrespectful to make eye contact with a teacher, so looking down must not be interpreted as lack of attention. Because the students themselves direct the themes they are interested in, certain cultural interests and taboos are automatically accommodated.

Tutors are further counseled that in order to preserve the all-accepting character of the public library experience, the tutor cannot impose his or her own values on the learners. Sometimes this is very difficult for them.

With the opening of the Flushing Library in June 1998, Queens Library set a new standard for Adult Learning Centers, particularly for a polyglot community such as Flushing. Joel L. Swerdlow, writing in the August 1999 *National Geographic,* truly captured the character of the Flushing Library in his article "Tale of Three Cities." "An English conversation group is meeting on the lower level, and I sit in for a while. Some of the students describe New York as a school, where they learn about survival in America. 'If I can make it there, I'll make it anywhere,' says one, quoting a 1977 show tune. I join an English-language class in another room, where I sit between an opera singer from Shanghai and a botanist from Uzbekistan. Unable to find work as a botanist because he does not yet speak English well, Yuzef helps his two sons with their jewelry manufacturing business."

The Adult Learning Center at Flushing was a priority in planning for the new building. The facility includes a separate classroom for ESOL instruction; a separate tutoring room, so activities there will not interfere with the conversation groups; individual work areas for multimedia learning; and computer workstations for self-paced learning. We believe the Flushing Adult Learning Center is a model for the way in which adult learners can be served, and is a visible testament to how important we feel adult literacy is to the mission of the library.

The Public Library Commitment

We have made a significant commitment to adult learning at the Queens Library, as many other public libraries have done. But a public library does not have to provide instruction or have learning centers to make a commitment to eradicating illiteracy in its community. Public libraries can be involved in the following ways:

Literacy instruction is often a collaborative effort as it has developed in the United States. Three in four direct-provider libraries (78.1%) collaborate with an outside agency or program to provide adult literacy tutoring or instruction. Of these, two-thirds (68.0%) partner with a volunteer literacy tutoring group such as Literacy Volunteers of America or Laubach Literacy International. Among the other library partners are school districts (38.1%), local community college/technical schools (34.0%) and other community-based organizations (38.9%)—*Survey Executive Summary,* p. 2

Public libraries are active providers of adult literacy programs and services, as indicated by the percent that reported providing each program or service listed below (= 1,067):

Maintain information about literacy services in the community	94.1%
Refer potential students to adult literacy programs	93.4%
Have/provide space in your building(s) that is used for adult literacy tutoring of instruction	83.9%
Provide literacy print materials for new adult readers/learners	83.1%
Conduct library tours/orientation for literacy students or tutors/instructors	66.8%
Develop and distribute publicity about providers of literacy services (e.g., production of brochures, newsletters, or audiovisual materials)	38.6%
Publicize the problem of low literacy (e.g., public hearings, informational programs, library displays, news coverage)	32.4%
Directly participate in a program to deliver tutoring or instruction in adult literacy (lend professional staff, library materials, or financial support to the instructional process)	30.1%

—Survey, pp. 4–5

Be knowledgeable of the conditions of literacy in their service communities and gather information and facts concerning literacy status, service providers, and delivery systems that are available to adult learners. Reference librarians, children's librarians, and readers' advisors are key referral agents to such services on behalf of library customers.

Develop collections of educational materials, including ones designed especially for adults at low reading levels and containing books that parents can read to their children. Collections should include teachers' manuals and tutoring guides.

Provide meeting room space for tutor instruction, local learning councils, and learner instruction provided by other organizations.

Participate in community coalitions that focus on adult learning and family literacy. Actively advocate approaches that recognize the condition of illiteracy in the community and work to find community solutions. Work with adult schools, community colleges, and private providers to ensure that all in need have the opportunity to be served.

Provide instruction to adult learners in basic English and English for Speakers of Other Languages, using computer-aided instruction and one-on-one or small-group tutoring. This is the highest level of involvement for a public library.

Make sure that every adult in a learning program receives orientation to the public library and its services, and instruction in how to access and use information, facts, and knowledge for personal empowerment.

Reaching out as we do in public library literacy programs, we want to draw people into public libraries for the rest of their lives. Public libraries are uniquely qualified to provide literacy instruction because, while the focus of other institutions may change over time, libraries are all about literacy and they always will be, whether that literacy is applied to paper, to electronic formats, or to some other medium we haven't yet dreamed of. And we'll be here to provide it in English, or any other language that our customers need.

■ 15 ■

Literacy and Technology

Thinking through the Process

SARAH NIXON and TIM PONDER

The purpose of this chapter is to describe key issues regarding the integration of computer technology into adult literacy programs. "It's not having computers that is important, it is how they are used."[1] Everyone is aware of the financial commitment that is needed to integrate computer technology into an adult literacy program; however, few realize the importance of revising a program's philosophical and educational commitment to include computer technology. Strommen and Lincoln state: "What is needed is a guiding philosophy that suggests principled changes in the curriculum and effective uses of technology as part of these changes."[2] Disregarding this component could prove expensive—in more ways than one—in the long run.

Below we will address several issues of importance that programs need to consider whether they are contemplating adding computer technology to the program or if it already exists. These issues are divided into five categories: (1) program philosophy, (2) curriculum and instruction, (3) software, (4) e-mail, and (5) the Internet. Each section begins with a few reflective questions that are meant to help guide you through the thought process of integrating computer technology into your literacy program.

Program Philosophy

Is the use of computer technology a part of your program's philosophy? Is the use of computer technology a part of your mission statement? How is computer technology integrated into your philosophy and mission statement?

An adult literacy program's philosophy and mission statement address issues that lie at the heart of the program. When major changes occur within the structure of the program, these changes should be reflected in the philosophy and mission statement. Often, educational institutions jump on the computer technology bandwagon without thinking through all aspects of the program that will be affected. Simple availability and use of computers will not ensure student success.[3]

Key stakeholders in the literacy program—including administrators, teachers, tutors, and learners—need to openly discuss their concepts of *why* computer technology should be integrated and *how* this should occur. To effectively integrate computers into a program and into the curriculum, a great deal of time in planning, reviewing, and evaluating needs to be taken. Administrators have to decide how teachers and tutors will be trained to use the new technology and software. It is important for teachers and tutors to reflect on how they envision incorporating computer technology into their curricula and daily lessons. And the bottom line is student achievement: how will administrators, teachers, and tutors ensure that learners will make satisfactory progress? How will computer technology help to meet and address their needs?

As a starting point, administrators can survey teachers and tutors on their beliefs, knowledge, and classroom use of computer technology. The information gleaned from this survey can help them consider what type of in-service workshops are needed to educate and update their teachers and tutors, and to obtain an idea of how teachers use or will be using computer technology with their students. Niederhauser and Stoddart conducted a statewide survey regarding teachers' usage of technology in their classrooms and found that teachers fell into two camps of thought: (1) those who believed that computers are tools for students to use to gather, examine, and display information; and (2) those who believed that computers are teaching machines that can be used to present information, offer immediate feedback, and track student progress.[4] The study established:

> Teachers' beliefs about effective uses of computers are closely linked with their use of computers in the classroom. Teachers who use more open-ended, constructivist type software with their students believe that computers can be used more effectively as a tool for student construction of

knowledge, while teachers who use more traditional behaviorist types of software believe that computers are effective as teaching machines.[5]

Administrators need to be aware that multiple realities face educators regarding the use and implementation of computers, and critically think through and discuss these new realities ahead of time.

Curriculum and Instruction

Does your program's curriculum integrate the use of computer technology? How are teachers and tutors using and implementing computer technology into the curriculum?

Administrators, teachers, and tutors must be specific about their goals for integrating computer technology into the curriculum. Computer use should be meaningful and purposeful, not an activity that is conducted for a change of pace. Effective computer use focuses on achievement of concrete gains with specific written objectives. Teachers need to plan computer sessions and ask themselves, "Does this time on the computer address the direct needs and skills of my students?" Computer time should not just be a time for free exploration; students need direction and they need to work toward enhancing specific skills.

Two modes of instruction can be implemented: (1) meaning-oriented reading and writing activities such as keeping journals, researching, creating newsletters or flyers, reading articles or books, or (2) targeted direct instruction in word identification or strategies for reading fluency and comprehension. It should be noted, though, that moving from a teacher-centered focus to a student-centered focus will not automatically increase students' success. Computers are a good source of motivation and can raise self-esteem, but they can also be used for the achievement of actual skill objectives.

Another important issue for administrators and teachers to consider is the use of small-group instruction on the computer. Learning is a social process and students learn more effectively when they are collaborating with others. Vygotsky believed that what students can do together is a better indicator of their development than what they could do alone. "The Vygotskian perspective enables us to see that collaborative tasks requiring data generation, planning, and management can provide another set of valuable experiences" for learners.[6]

Several researchers concur with Forman and Cazden. Hoyles, Healy, and Sutherland reported the dramatic change in the quality as well as quantity of peer group discussions when students worked together in small groups on the computer. Other researchers have observed and reported on the power of student collaboration and cooperation during the use of newer, more learner-centered software. Harel and Papert and Wepner observed that students took more responsibility for their learning when they were interacting with learner-centered software. Also, researchers have reported that writing using computer-mediated communication was beneficial for the lower-ability writer.

It should be noted, however, that students seldom interact with a computer in the way they will with other people in a classroom—even when computers are strategically placed in the room; therefore, it is the responsibility of the teacher to stress the importance of collaborative computer work and create lessons that will ensure this type of social interaction. The goal is to create a "community of writers" where talk influences writing as well as the social fabric of the class. Teachers can expand students' writing opportunities to include publishing, such as the production of a program newsletter, as well as cards, signs, and posters.

Software

What types of software programs does your program use? How does this software complement your curriculum and instruction? Is the software compatible with your program philosophy?

Administrators, teachers, and tutors need to discuss the congruency of computer software with their curricula, taking into consideration that computer-based reading instruction is not meant to replace reading instruction but rather to supplement it. Case and Truscott state:

> Simply using a computer to do what could be done by conventional means will not necessarily result in increased achievement. Additionally, it would be unwise to have students complete activities on the computer that are not congruent with and at the same caliber of other pedagogically sound classroom activities.[7]

Each literacy program should implement a system of previewing and evaluating effective software that includes the learners as well as the teachers, tutors, and administrators. Software should be chosen carefully, especially drill-and-skill software. "Technology only has a place in the classroom when the software used is based on educationally sound practices and is congruent with how reading is taught today."[8]

E-mail

Is the use of e-mail a part of your program's curriculum and instruction? How is the use of e-mail integrated into the curriculum and instruction?

The use of e-mail as a tool for improving writing is well documented. Several studies investigated the use of computers and the writing process, such as e-mail writing partners and creating classroom newsletters. Studies reported that students of all ages and abilities enjoyed writing more when they used a word-processing program. Many researchers also reported an increase in quality of writing by computer users.

E-mail-based projects are a relatively easy way to get involved with technology. E-mail provides chances for literacy learning in two ways: it makes learning social, and students actively use literacy in meaningful ways, thus creating authentic situations for reading and writing. Learners can practice writing and write to authentic audiences. Learners can find their own voice and obtain new cultural knowledge. E-mail provides an opportunity for adult learners to meet people who are very different from them and hold different beliefs; it brings the outside world into their lives.

The use of e-mail has been used successfully to facilitate discussion outside and inside the classroom as well as to increase communication between students. E-mail can help learners who might be shy and reserved in a class setting to participate in an online discussion where they are more apt to speak out and speak up. E-mail also provides the opportunity for learners to think and reflect before replying, and offers repeated readings if needed. And, most importantly for adult learners, e-mail provides students with the opportunity to become familiar with a mode of communication that is increasingly a part of what it means to be literate.

Internet

Is the use of the Internet and the World Wide Web a part of your program's curriculum and instruction? How is it integrated into the curriculum and instruction?

The Internet provides a plethora of up-to-date information and abundant resources for teachers of struggling readers and writers. Collections of lesson plans are available online, and professional organizations provide websites and online newsletters. Administrators, teachers, and students can join online discussion groups; teachers can find avenues to publish student-created materials and display students' work to a wider audience. Teachers and students can publish online or create a class/program web page.

Karchmer suggests that teachers "transform" the Internet and its usefulness to make it work for them, their students, and their particular needs. Teachers who "adapt" technology to meet their needs, their students' needs, and the program's needs have "figured out where the Internet fits into their curriculum, how it can help them construct new visions for literacy and learning, and how they can share this knowledge with other educators and students." [9]

Literacy programs that use or plan on using the Internet as an instructional tool need to take into consideration several issues. Much of the information found on the Internet through random searches will either not be relevant to the subject at hand or the reading level will be too difficult for adult learners. Teachers and tutors should seek out sites that are not at the learner's frustration level; therefore, prior previewing and teacher planning time is necessary to find sites that match curriculum goals and learning levels of students. Teachers and tutors need to evaluate selected sites for reading level, importance of material and information, user friendliness of the website, and information presentation. Teachers should bookmark these sites to help facilitate their learners' searches.

The integration of technology into an adult literacy program hinges as much on process and planning as it does on hardware and software. Reflecting on how technology fits into a program's educational plan and philosophy is essential to the successful use of technology as a teaching and learning tool for adult literacy.

NOTES

1. H. McDonald and L. Ingvarson, *Free at Last? Teachers, Computers and Independent Learning.* Paper presented at the annual meeting of the American Educational Research Association, San Francisco, Calif., 1995, p. 3. (ERIC Document Reproduction Service No. ED 389 278)

2. E. F. Strommen and B. Lincoln, "Constructivism, Technology, and the Future of Classroom Learning," *Education and Urban Society* 24 (1992): 466–76.

3. L. D. Labbo and D. Reinking. "Negotiating the Multiple Realities of Technology in Literacy Research and Instruction," *Reading Research Quarterly* 35 (1999): 478–92.

4. D. S. Niederhauser and T. Stoddart, *Teachers' Perspectives on Computer-Assisted Instruction: Transmission versus Construction of Knowledge.* Paper presented at the

annual meeting of the American Educational Research Association, New Orleans, La., 1994. (ERIC Document Reproduction Service No. ED 374 116)

5. Ibid., p. 11.

6. L. S. Vygotsky, *Mind in Society: The Development of Higher Psychological Processes* (M. Cole, V. John-Steiner, S. Schribner, and E. Souberman, eds.) (Cambridge, Mass.: Harvard University Press, 1978).

7. C. Case and D. M. Truscott, "The Lure of Bells and Whistles: Choosing the Best Software to Support Reading Instruction," *Reading & Writing Quarterly* 15 (1999): 364.

8. Ibid. p. 362

9. R. A. Karchmer, "Understanding Teachers' Perspectives of Internet Use in the Classroom: Implications for Teacher Education and Staff Development," *Reading & Writing Quarterly* 16 (2000): 82.

REFERENCES

Anderson, J., and Andrea Lee. "Literacy Teachers Learning a New Literacy: A Study of the Use of Electronic Mail in a Reading Education Class." *Reading Research and Instruction* 34 (1995): 222–38.

Baer, V. "Computers as Composition Tools: A Case Study of Student Attitudes." *Journal of Computer-Based Instruction* 15 (1988): 144–48.

Balajthy, E. "The Effects of Teacher Purpose on Achievement Gains." *Reading & Writing Quarterly* 16, no. 3 (July 2000): 289–94.

Beach, R., and Lundell, D. "Early Adolescents' Use of Computer-Mediated Communication in Writing and Reading." In *Handbook of Literacy and Technology: Transformations in a Post-Typographic World.* Mahwah, N.J.: Erlbaum Assoc., 1998.

Bernhardt, S., S. Edwards, and P. Wojahn. "Teaching College Composition with Computers: A Program Evaluation Study." *Written Communication* 6 (1989): 108–33.

Brady, L. "Overcoming Resistance: Computers in the Writing Classroom." *Computers and Composition* 7 (1990): 21–33.

Case, C., and D. M. Truscott. "The Lure of Bells and Whistles: Choosing the Best Software to Support Reading Instruction." *Reading & Writing Quarterly* 15 (1999): 361–69.

Forman, E. A., and C. B. Cazden. "Exploring Vygotskian Perspectives in Education: The Cognitive Value of Peer Interaction." In *Theoretical Models and Processes of Reading,* 4th ed. Newark, Del.: International Reading Association, 1994.

Hartman, K., C. Neuwirth, S. Kiesler, L. Sproull, C. Cochran, M. Palmquist, and D. Zubrow. "Patterns of Social Interaction and Learning to Write: Some Effects of Network Technologies." *Written Communication* 8 (1991): 79–113.

Hoyles, C., L. Healy, and R. Sutherland. "Patterns of Discussion between Pupil Pairs in Computer Environments and Non-computer Environments." *Journal of Computer Assisted Learning* ⁻ ⌐1): 210–28.

Karchmer, R. A. "Understanding Teachers' Perspectives of Internet Use in the Classroom: Implications for Teacher Education and Staff Development." *Reading & Writing Quarterly* 16 (2000): 81–85.

Labbo, L. D., and D. Reinking. "Negotiating the Multiple Realities of Technology in Literacy Research and Instruction." *Reading Research Quarterly* 35 (1999): 478–92.

Mackinson, J. A., and J. K. Peyton. "Interactive Writing on a Computer Network: A Teacher/Researcher Collaboration." In *Delicate Balances: Collaborative Research in Language Education.* Urbana, Ill.: National Council of Teachers of English, 1993.

McDonald, H., and L. Ingvarson. *Free at Last? Teachers, Computers and Independent Learning.* Paper presented at the annual meeting of the American Educational Research Association, San Francisco, Calif., 1995. (ERIC Document Reproduction Service No. ED 389 278)

Miller, L. "Multimedia and Young Children's Symbol-Weaving." *Reading & Writing Quarterly* 14, no. 1 (Jan.-Mar. 1998): 109–14.

Moore, M. Computers Can Enhance Transactions between Readers and Writers. *Reading Teacher* 42 (1989): 608–11.

Niederhauser, D. S., and T. Stoddart. *Teachers' Perspectives on Computer-Assisted Instruction: Transmission versus Construction of Knowledge.* Paper presented at the annual meeting of the American Educational Research Association, New Orleans, La., 1994. (ERIC Document Reproduction Service No. ED 374 116)

Rosenbluth, G., and W. Reed. "The Effects of Writing-Process-Based Instruction and Word Processing on Remedial and Accelerated 11th Graders." *Computers in Human Behavior* 8 (1992): 120–42.

Sanaoui, R., and S. Lapkin. "A Case Study of an ESL Senior Secondary Course Integrating Computer Networking." *Canadian Modern Language Review* 48 (1992): 225–52.

Schwartz, J. "Using an Electronic Network to Play the Scales of Discourse." *English Journal* 79 (1990): 16–24.

Spaulding, C., and D. Lake. *Interactive Effects of Computer Network and Student Characteristics on Students' Writing and Collaborating.* Presented at the annual meeting of the American Education Research Association, Chicago, Ill., April 1991. (ERIC Document Reproduction Service No. ED 329 966)

Strommen, F., and B. Lincoln. "Constructivism, Technology, and the Future of Classroom Learning." *Education and Urban Society* 24 (1992): 466–76.

Tao, L., and D. Reinking. "E-mail and Literacy Education." *Reading & Writing Quarterly* 16, no. 2 (April 2000): 169–74.

Vygotsky, L. S. *Mind in Society: The Development of Higher Psychological Processes.* (M. Cole, V. John-Steiner, S. Scribner, and E. Souberman, eds.). Cambridge, Mass.: Harvard University Press, 1978.

▪ 16 ▪

The Brooklyn Public Library and Technology for Literacy

SUSAN K. O'CONNOR and DEBBIE GUERRA

As you walk into any one of the six Brooklyn Public Library Learning Centers you enter a learning environment. You'll find iMacs loaded with word processors, a database and spreadsheet, and creativity tools, such as Storybook Weaver, Kid Pix, Printshop Deluxe, and Print Artist, as well as a few Internet browsers. Poems, anthologies, summer reading databases, and autobiographies cover the bulletin boards. When students walk in, they retrieve their disks, start programs, locate files, and get down to work. You might find students surfing the Web, scanning family photographs, or printing a greeting card. How did we get here and how long did it take?

Nine years ago our computer rooms were quiet spaces where students worked in isolation on Apple IIe computers loaded with drill-and-practice software. Computer aides did the work of booting software and closing programs. The only printouts were more drill-and-practice exercises that students finished for homework.

In 1992, when our Apple IIe's wore out, we applied for and received a Library Services and Construction Act (LSCA) grant to replace them. We had no idea that we were setting into motion a force that would change the ways we viewed our students, the learning process, and ourselves. "Learning to use computers can change the way we learn everything else." This statement, by John Sculley, in the introduction to Seymour Papert's

Mindstorms: Children, Computers, and Powerful Ideas (Basic Books, 1999), proved to be a rule that we would rediscover, to our amazement, time and again.

An End and a Beginning

While we were preparing the LSCA proposal, we consulted with the staff at Playing to Win, an innovative storefront technology center in Harlem started by Antonia Stone. They pointed us in a new direction. They urged us to purchase application tools instead of educational software. Skeptical at first—could adult literacy students use word processors?—we included the application tools in the grant. Something else happened to us at the same time.

Computers entered our workplace. Although some of us had worked on word processors using a DOS program, maneuvering around a screen using a mouse was new. We all got our first lessons in what it felt like to be illiterate, and it was scary. However, this situation also provided us with fresh experiences and insights into how adults learn.

As we worked on our new PCs, we realized three things. First, that learning happened naturally because we were involved in activities that were important and useful to us. Next, learning was a noisy, collaborative process that involved sharing information, asking questions, and listening. Finally, learning didn't happen in a neat, orderly sequence. We didn't learn how to use Microsoft Word by following an instruction manual, and we didn't need drill-and-practice to retain skills.

Our active learning experiences provided a sharp contrast to what we provided students in the computer rooms. We saw that the drill-and-practice software required learning information out of a real-world context, and working in isolation within a preset curriculum. It did not tap the power of the computer to find, sort, and process information. Realizing that the computer was an important source of information and means of communication, we had to figure out how to immediately assist learners in mastering the use of technology.

We discarded all drill-and-practice software and redesigned the learning environment to support active learning. Now we had to develop a new curricular model that supported students using technology as they learned to read, write, and use information. We needed approaches that modeled the sort of questioning and problem solving we engaged in as we learned.

Creating a Risk-Free Environment

We changed the layout of our technology labs, emulating our own workspaces. We grouped computers so that students could easily talk, share information, and lean over and help each other. Students were consulted about what worked for them and became a part of the change process, reviewing software and providing us with feedback along the way.

We steered students toward articulating questions and seeking information, and away from the belief that learning is about finding the right answer. Lack of information and mistakes didn't need to be hidden. They were important points that launched new directions of learning, sharing, and growing.

Technology Supports Writing

In 1991 we set up writing groups using a writing process model developed by Lucy Calkins at Teachers College, Columbia University. Students joined writing groups and wrote down their stories, yet putting pen to paper continued to be a difficult and slow process.

The LC2 computers were purchased with the LSCA grant and loaded with new word processors. They were the first real tool that made drafting, revision, and editing easy. Functions such as cut and paste, the delete key, and spellcheck were irresistible. Learners committed more and more hours to working on computers. The volume of published products increased steadily each year.

Desktop publishing gave learners the experience of being insiders in the writing world. By including graphics and experimenting with text formats, they could publish work. They were proud. They were computer literate. The Writing Center by the Learning Company was and remains the most popular word processor. Even our most reluctant writers were drawn toward creating short pieces enhanced with graphics. Everyone learned important lessons about the world of print: how text and graphics work together to create meaning, and to enhance, enlarge, and communicate ideas.

From there students began to explore creativity tools to design and present their stories and research. Students used Print Artist and Print Shop Deluxe to create covers, banners, certificates, and greeting cards. They used Kid Pix to design original art. Creating pictures freed students from the constraints of written communication and gave them new ways of thinking and communicating ideas. Internet sites increased the availability of images connected to the events and people students were writing about.

> Mark learned how to move a picture from the Writing Center to Kid Pix to modify it. He was very proud of this and most of the students he showed were amazed. They wanted to do it too. Having more confidence allows Mark to take more chances. Now he writes longer pieces.—a computer aide

Desktop publishing provided a larger audience for students' work, while stimulating new reasons to write. As students were drawn into the delicious possibilities of desktop publishing their confidence grew. Staff saw the possibilities of engaging students at a deeper level through projects.

Project-Based Learning

We began using a project-based approach in order to help learners organize their learning around themes that interested them. Thus, the projects engaged learners over longer periods of time. Projects moved them into deeper levels of thought and provided new opportunities to process information and develop skills. Internet sites made it easy to find information and creativity tools helped students turn their research into finished products.

Projects included newsletters, travel guides, family albums, poetry anthologies, children's stories, book-review databases, family trees, cookbooks, celebrity research, topics in the news, pie chart results of student-conducted surveys, family stories, and projects for black and women's history months.

> My students created family albums. They wrote stories, created databases compiling information on family members and created a family tree. The final part of the project was creating the family tree. Students used Kid Pix because they enjoyed working with this fun software. One learner who quickly got the hang of drawing worked beside me as a co-teacher to help the other students create their trees. This was a great motivator to get other students into the computer room because the students who worked on their family trees told everyone. Now others want to do it!—a tutor

As we moved into the writing process and project-based learning, we evaluated our instructional model. Projects require a different orientation on the part of the facilitator. There is no set curriculum. Projects are open-ended and gather momentum as they move forward.

> I worked with a group of four beginning readers on a newsletter project which took them through word processing, graphics, collecting data through interviews, using a database and creating a pie chart. I really didn't have much of a "plan" for the project in its early stages because I was a novice computer user myself and didn't know what to expect. It turned out that the more application programs the students were exposed to, the more questions they asked, and each step of the project evolved naturally from the last.—a computer aide

We redesigned the computer aide training. We sought to teach computer aides how to facilitate writing and help the development of information literacy skills through discussion and questions. Aides learned how to talk people through problems without grabbing the mouse. Modeling thinking and problem-solving processes became essential. They were there to empower students to find their own solutions.

A New Tutor-Training Model

Where did tutors fit into these changes? We needed tutors who could trust us when we asked them to trade off a tidy curriculum for an active learning model, tutors who could forge cohesive groups and were good listeners. We were searching for people who shared our passion for learning and would believe in the students' potential, even if they didn't see it right away. We needed tutors who could help learners use a variety of technological tools, from word processor to scanner. We designed a pretraining orientation where we asked prospective tutors to share active learning experiences. Listening to their stories helped us select the best candidates.

Technology has had a great impact on the eight-session tutor training. Laptops were added to the training to facilitate the tutors' exploration of the writing process. Tutors now must work together on projects to get firsthand experience of group dynamics. They learn how to draw out the learners' emerging voices through listening and feedback. They are given an overview of the technology labs and a chance to create a product using the software.

I strongly encourage tutors to try learning with multimedia. The passion my students developed for this experience is irreplaceable. Just a few days after publishing the book, I found members of the group back on the CD-ROMs exploring and reading. The group asked me when they were going to start the next project. Even though we've had a hot, muggy summer, attendance has been 86%.—a tutor

Getting Connected with the Internet

Getting connected was a long process that started with an invitation to join the National Center on Adult Literacy's Adult Literacy Technology Innovation Network (ALTIN) project. In 1994 we joined what would turn out to be an exhilarating exploration of new possibilities in using technology as a learning tool, a chance to network with innovative organizations across the country, and to open our first two Internet accounts.

We used the Internet to communicate with each other. Learning groups held online book chats, joined key pal projects. As learners became more familiar with the Internet, they used it increasingly as an information tool. Today all the centers are connected to high-speed T1 lines, iMacs are in place, and modems are suddenly an item from a bygone era.

Building Staff Development into the Grant Process

Staff development was the key to real change. Goals and a vision for technology use were clearly communicated to all staff members. We knew that if tutors and students were to use technology, all staff members had to be computer literate. Therefore, by necessity, the money for staff development was written into every grant in order to assure that our vision became a reality.

At the same time, we understood that becoming proficient technology users would take a while. Training needed to be flexible, designed to meet everyone's needs. From formal training in application software to informal computer clubs, staff were provided with a menu of choices for coming together and exploring new tools in a nonjudgmental, fun environment. We explored the software our students used and created our own stories using The Writing Center's picture folder, and Storybook Weaver. Creating a literate environment demands active learning.

Technology Support

We've had our problems: system crashes, computers slowing down, and worse. Our software had overextended the computers. We bought additional time with external hard drives, but this was only a Band-Aid approach. We sought and were awarded a Lila Wallace-Reader's Digest Literacy in Libraries Across America grant, and we bought Macintosh G3s. They were *so* fast that they couldn't work with our software. We had to buy new software. Then the LC2s wore out.

Maintaining and upgrading equipment have been an ongoing challenge. The reason we survived is because we are a learning organization with a flexible staff. Their ability to troubleshoot problems, or just to clearly articulate them to the tech support team has helped us not dissolve in the face of sad Macs.

One thing is certain, the adult learners have been in that computer room the entire time and have watched staff share information, work collaboratively, articulate problems, and try a variety of approaches to solve them. They've seen staff accomplish results by *not* quitting or blaming themselves or walking off in defeat. They've witnessed what adult learners can do when they don't give up.

Measuring Change

We assessed our first technology grant by comparing the number of hours students used the computer room before and after installation of the Macs. During the first six months, computer usage had increased more than 300 percent, from 3,746 hours in 1993 to 12,242 hours in 1994. Since computer use was not mandated, it became obvious that this experience was increasingly valued.

Initially, we used a questionnaire to probe the impact of computer literacy on learners' lives. We learned that as students developed their new technology skills, their attitudes toward technology and the way they perceived themselves as learners changed. Students were using cash machines, buying computers for their homes, and felt more in touch with their children.

> I've been using the computer for almost a year now and every time I sit in front of it, it's an exciting challenge for me. When I was first introduced to the computer it seemed complicated and technical. Now I approach it with

confidence. Anyone with a will to learn can and should challenge themselves to learn the computer. It prepares you for success in this world of technology.—a student

We examined the work of the students and talked to them about their writing. Learners indicated that using the computer enabled them to write with ease because they could easily enter the text, move things around, delete words, and fix spelling. On the advice of Loren McGrail of Literacy South, a Lila Wallace-Reader's Digest Fund technical advisor, we decided to create a writing rubric to show the acceleration of students' ability to write using technology. This was completed in 1998. Now the writing rubric is a standard assessment tool for the Brooklyn Public Library Literacy Program.

Toward a New Confidence

Nonreaders can quickly learn how to navigate menus, use the mouse, find documents, use the keyboard, save, and print. Computer aides reported that students who were previously silent were suddenly beginning to talk to each other, specifically to share their competencies and support each other's learning.

> Many of these students always thought of themselves as being unable to do anything. When they come here and discover that they can write, be creative, it's often because the computer is a liberating learning experience. They not only learn that they can do things, but they begin to see themselves as people who just may have creative ability.—a computer aide

The Library as a Learning Place

The library is a nontraditional, nonclassroom setting. When adults join us they set their own learning goals, plan projects to pursue those goals in meaningful formats, and access information through a variety of resources. Our goal is to help students become lifelong learners who will turn to the library in the future. We want to be both a personal and a community resource that supports learners with access to the best tools.

Nine years ago our program was closer to a traditional classroom, where the tutor was the holder of knowledge, captain of the curriculum, asker of questions. As we moved toward realizing our potential as a library program, we moved away from that model. We utilize trained tutors, but it is the learner who decides the goals and formulates the questions. The staff and tutors are there to suggest paths to information, model literate behaviors, and lend a helping hand.

Where to Next?

We just opened a new learning center in Flatbush. This center reflects the future because technology is integrated throughout the center. There is a computer lab and wireless communications. Groups can meet anywhere in the facility and be able to utilize laptops and the Internet without being plugged into a wall outlet. This allows freedom of movement and perhaps a quieter space to be noisy!

The Brooklyn Public Library Literacy Program students have not only crossed the digital divide but they have built bridges and towers to lifelong learning. Their success and positive word of mouth keeps the adults arriving at our doors and, as a library, the door is always open.

> After five months . . . I am able to master the computer. I can work on it more comfortably and without any assistance and it feels wonderful. I don't feel intimidated by computers anymore. I can select any program I want and work on it.—a student

Students' Stories

Winston George
Coney Island Learning Center (excerpt)

What I will like to do is to be able to read a lot more. I know a little about the computer. So I will like to read and write some more. Some time I try to do a little reading on my job. And each time I get at home I try to do a little on the computer. It help me with my reading and writing. . . . I like to come to the Coney Island Learning Center to learn how to read and write. . . . I came to this learning center on this date, 8/16/97. Not knowing how to read or write it became impossible for me to get around by myself in a big city like New York with only sign all around you and you cannot read them. . . . . You have two choice. One, you can sit back and cry about your condition. Or you can go and look for some help. The choice is yours. So do something about it. It will not hurt you. . . . One, I had to get rid of my pride. The pride that tell you that you are too old for this reading and writing business. Two, I had to forget what people will say about me. Three, think about the help you can get. Make a try. Go for it, you will make it. The first day I came to the learning center I was very much afraid. But when I met with the staff all the fear went away from me. . . . So for some of you that cannot read and write, and you heard about this story. It will change your way of thinking. And it will make you think positive. I tell you what. Take a chance you will not regret it. Because it happen to me. I was there and i know how it feel, not to be able to read and write. This is a true story, by the writer.

Jackline Robert
Eastern Parkway Learning Center

I came to the library's literacy program because I wanted to improved on my reading and writing. I stayed at the library's literacy program because I find what I was looking for and it's very interesting to me. I learn to read about stories, newspapers, and to interview my classmates. Then I learn to write about what I read and by looking at pictures in a book and write about what I saw in it. That's what I learn from my tutor and I also learn to use the computer. I change because I am always doing a little reading, writing and Miss Maryane and my tutor Ray told me I am doing well in my reading, writing and especially in my spellings. Yes there is a lot I can say because the tutors are very kind, patient and careful about their students.

Dumel Renois
Eastern Parkway Learning Center

I come to Brooklyn Public Library to learn how to read and write. Then one day, I can help my children with their homework. Before I come I thought for me it's too late. But after my childhood memories, I say to myself I should study day and night and then one day my dream could become true. Few months later, I have a dream, then one day I will write a book about my family life story. I thank God for all the good tutors who help us to read and write, and God blessed them all.

Cheniqua Peets
Eastern Parkway Learning Center

I came to the library, I have problems with reading and writing. I changed a lot with the help of tutors. I pray that my dream will come true. I know that reading is fundamental. When I came to learning center I was so shy to face people. Reading a book was so hard. By going to the library they make me feel so special.

George L. S. Brown
Bedford Learning Center (excerpt)

I stay with the literacy program, because I want to better myself and learn more about me and my surroundings. So that I can get the best job and position in life. I would like to be able to have something that I can call my own. To have something that I can leave so that people can remember my name for a long time. This will enable them to say that George L. S. Brown was here.

17

Computer Skills and Literacy

CAROL MORRIS

"E-mail is a wonderful thing to know. It gave me an opening to contact family and friends." "I like using the computer because of the things that computers are now changing." "Using the computer program Typing Tutor helped me learn how to type. This experience helped me get a second job this summer." "I like using the Internet because it helps me find things and plan vacations."

Are these quotations from a computer class? Comments from a computer class for senior citizens? Evaluations from a technology conference? Statements by adult new readers? Which one applies? The above statements are credited to adults attending the Lake County Literacy Program that is a coalition of the Waukegan Public Library, the College of Lake County, and Literacy Volunteers of Lake County. These adults became computer users because they were offered the opportunities and were shown the possibilities.

The Lake County Literacy Program (LCLP) has provided volunteer, tutor-based instruction for adults since 1986. Most individuals receiving instruction are new readers and writers, reading below the third-grade level as measured on standardized tests. Not so long ago many adult new readers thought that computers and the Internet were tools other people used, not something an individual who struggles with reading and writing would consider as an instrument for improving one's skills or as a source for information. For a large number of adult learners those perceptions have changed.

Literacy at the Mall

In 1996, with funding provided by the Lila Wallace-Reader's Digest Fund, the Lake County Literacy Program opened the Adult Learning Center at a local mall in Waukegan, Illinois. Initially the learning center housed six computers. Two of them were new, the remaining four were donated personal computers equipped with Windows 3.1. Available software included Typing Tutor, Basic Math Skills, Learning 2000, Language Tune-Up Kit, and Vocabulary Connections. As time progressed, the four older computers were slowly replaced with five newer computers until all came with Windows 95, sound, and Internet availability. The number of software programs grew from five to approximately forty different programs.

Computers are intended to supplement instruction rather than replace volunteer tutors, instructors, or staff. Students and tutors were slowly introduced to computers and the Internet by staff. Staff developed a simple questionnaire to determine learners' interests and needs, which facilitated the purchasing of new software. Prior to purchase, the software was previewed by students, tutors, and staff, if possible. Once the software was on-site, staff would sit with the learners and assist them in navigating the new programs. Staff also developed an "Easy In-Easy Out" guide for each of the programs and a list of the various skills taught, if the software was intended for remedial or instructional purposes. Both adjuncts were essential for tutors and staff who were not computer users. A software "catalog" was created by staff. This catalog lists the skills addressed in each software program, cost and publisher of the software, and the area of interest, e.g., history, phonics, or math.

Introduction to the Internet followed the same strategies: finding sites that were easy to read and navigate and of interest to adult learners. Most often the sites were bookmarked, eliminating the need for students to type in or paste in lengthy URLs. Recognizing the need for the Internet lessons or activities, staff developed Net Cards, which are the Internet lessons on a 4 x 5 card. The Net Card contains a reader-friendly site of interest to learners and comes with additional activities or lessons to complete while at the respective Internet site. Net Cards are available in sets of 15 on a range of topics, including sports, cars, family literacy, history, and student-written materials. The Net Cards have made using the Internet easier for adult learners, especially those new readers who are often accompanied by their tutors when using the Internet.

E-mail Is the Big Thing

For some learners, introducing e-mail was a selling point in using the Internet. Students were given e-mail addresses, primarily through Hot Mail. Once the learner got his/her own e-mail account, the next step was to find electronic pen pals, also known as "key pals," with whom the students could correspond. In theory the plan was excellent, however, keeping the key pals in contact became problematic. Students moved, lost their passwords, or forgot to check their e-mail on a regular basis. Some students' writing skills were better than others. After the initial contact some learners found it difficult to maintain correspondence saying, "I ran out of things to talk about." Other learners use e-mail on a very regular basis, primarily using it to write to family. One learner and his tutor write on a weekly basis to his family in Hawaii. The tutor serves as the "secretary" and writes what the student dictates.

In July 1998, the literacy office at the Waukegan Public Library (WPL) moved into its newly remodeled location within the library. The new locality came with a literacy learning center housing four new networked computers with Internet availability. Building on the success of the Adult Learning Center, literacy staff at the WPL began the process of ordering new software and advertising the literacy learning center to key personnel. Information about the library's learning center was sent to adult education instructors at the College of Lake County (community college), various community-based organizations, employment training centers, and the Salvation Army staff. Software aimed at non-English-speaking adult learners and those students interested in obtaining their GED appear to be the most used programs. Ultimate Phonics, a skill-building program directed at new readers, is also quite popular. Library employees also make use of the computer learning center, most often using Typing Tutor to build keyboarding skills and Master Pronunciation to improve English-speaking skills. The software catalog created earlier was very beneficial when purchasing new software for the library's literacy computer center.

Making Our Own E-tools

During the past four years staff have learned from the students with whom we work. Student preferences or "favorite software" sometimes surprised staff. The student liaison is now part of the software-selection process. Staff and tutors enjoy interactive, multimedia programs, which offer music, voices, text, and comprehensive reading activities. Adult learners seem to prefer software that is more remedial, or as the staff calls it, "drill and kill." Learners may spend an hour doing repetitive tasks such as learning the sounds of the consonants or all the short vowel sounds. Students want to work on skill-building lessons and those which are perceived as improving one's reading and writing deficits. Finding software at a comfortable reading level for new readers is a challenge. Most software written at the fourth-grade level and below is quite childish and the content is not of interest to adult students. In 1999, with funding provided by GTE through the Ohio Literacy Resource Center, staff created three CD-ROMs featuring student-written materials, photos, and voices. Reaction from adult learners has been phenomenal. They were excited to see themselves in digital print. Vocal responses included "This is so neat!" and "Can we do one on sports?" Creating our own CDs, although very time-consuming, appears to eliminate the need to search for commercially produced software written below the fourth-grade reading level with content of interest to adult learners. Staff know that adult learners' preferred reading material is other students' writings. The simplicity of structure and the contents make it very reader friendly.

Staff discovered a need to measure learner's technology skills, which led to the development of a pre- and post-computer-skills assessment tool. At the initial interview, students are asked to identify the various pieces of hardware. Most could name the screen, keyboard, and mouse. One learner, hesitant in his response, called the mouse a "rat." The interviewer replied, "That's close, it's in the same family, only it's called a mouse." Further technology exploration by staff generated a Technology Matrix, which correlates reading levels with expected computer skills. For instance, a competent reader should be able to use the Internet with little assistance, use word-processing software, and be able to save to a disk and print the document. New readers should, after some instruction, have some keyboarding skills, be able to use the Internet with assistance, and identify the parts of a computer.

Technology and all its accessories require a dedicated staff, both literacy and library personnel. This is important even more so when providing services for adult literacy students, many of whom are not typical library users. Library support staff may not understand the value of the Solitaire card game and may wish to remove it from the computer. However, it's a great way to teach mouse skills. Furthermore, it is extremely important to keep the whole library staff informed as to what's available in the literacy computer center. Adult Services staff need to know that library customers could take a practice GED test in the learning center or could review the citizenship test. Or history buffs could learn something about American history via the Apple Pie Music software.

Adult students, especially new readers, are becoming computer and Internet users. In a recent survey to document new learner accomplishments or achievements, adult learners enrolled in the Lake County Literacy Program reported that 17.6 percent of the respondents were using computers either at work or home and 11.7 percent indicated they were using the Internet at work or home.

As learners' computer and Internet skills grow, future plans for students include learning to use the digital camera and scanner, which will allow them to create flyers, learner newsletters, and other student-written materials. One learner is slated to teach a mini-photography class for fellow students. We hope students will create stories, essays, and poetry to accompany their photos. Technology offers unlimited possibilities for adult literacy students. Quoting John Wyatt, an adult new reader, "My most favorite thing is working on the computer. My progress is super so far. I am hoping for bigger and better things next semester, like the Internet where I can get information." Adult learners just need to be invited into the technology possibilities.

Student Writing about E-mail

About E-mail by Daniel Gaspar

E-mail is a wonderful thing to know. Whoever invented it, I want to tell you thank you very much. It gave me an opening to contact other family and friends and people. If you don't know how to use the e-mail you should ask your librarian, your tutor or friend because it opens up a lot of things for us to find out. I learned what's happening about the world.

I was able to make contact with all my family in Hawaii, Washington, New York, California, Oregon, Pennsylvania and Illinois. We sent pictures of my child to the family. I wrote to a well-known cookie man, the man with no name, Wally Amos (he's the man!). I wrote to Guitar Gavin from US 99, a radio jockey. I see him once in a while at a promotion at McDonald's for the radio station. He is a local brother from the big island, Hawaii. E-mail broadened my outlook with my wife's side of the family. We found out that her grandma is one of the Hatfield's (of the Hatfield's and McCoy's in Tennessee).

So you know what e-mail does for me. It is very important for people. I encourage you people to look forward to learning about e-mail. It's the most mind-opening thing to see the world.

Daniel Gaspar is an adult learner currently enrolled in the Lake County Literacy Program. He and his tutor, Teta Minuzzo, meet twice weekly to work on his reading and writing skills. Usually once a week they send e-mail to Daniel's family in Hawaii. Recently, after the birth of his daughter, they sent photos via the Internet to family and friends. In May 2000, Daniel received the Spotlight on Achievement Award presented by the Illinois Secretary of State and the Illinois Press Association in recognition of his commitment to learning and his giving back to the community. He is one of the Lake County Literacy Program's Learner Leaders.

▪ 18 ▪

Another Divide

Low-Literacy Adults and the New Technology

RANDALL WEAVER

Much has been written concerning the large number of Americans who are unable to participate in the technological, social, and economic revolution which has been created by the personal computer. Who does and who does not have access to computers is often explained in simple economic terms; underfunded schools and discrepancies in personal income are seen as major factors creating the digital divide. Those of us who work in the field of adult literacy know that there are other barriers that are separating our clients from the digital world.

While participating in a seminar in San Francisco, I had the pleasure of speaking with David Bolt, the producer of the PBS documentary called *The Digital Divide.* He happened to be moderating our panel discussion of this topic and I was impressed with his grasp of this important issue. He shared a story with me concerning my place of employment, the San Francisco Public Library.

It seems that Mr. Bolt had arrived at the library early one morning for a meeting and witnessed the spectacle of the Main Library's daily opening. A mad rush of patrons came charging through the doors and Bolt noticed that many appeared to be the same homeless street people whom he had passed by as he arrived. They all seemed to be in a great hurry to get somewhere in the library. He asked the librarian what they were so anxious to do. He was informed that they were rushing to get onto the many Internet Access Computers available free of charge in the library. He asked what they primarily used these computers for, and the librarian said that they mainly took advantage of free e-mail services in order to stay in contact with friends and family around the world. Witnessing this impressed upon him just how far-reaching and powerful the computer revolution has become. Even these unfortunate citizens who cannot afford a home are making use of the new technology thanks to the services of the public library. In this case, the digital divide is being effectively bridged. After hearing Bolt's commentary, I remember telling him that "these homeless patrons are really the lucky ones." Although these adults are not able to afford their own personal computers, they are able to take advantage of the new technology. They can decode the written information found on the computer and share their thoughts with others around the world. Just one floor above them in the library, adults are struggling daily to improve their reading and writing skills in order to do the same. For these men and women enrolled in Project READ, there is yet another divide.

Project READ

Project READ, the adult literacy program of the San Francisco Public Library, has been providing free one-on-one tutoring and small group instruction to English-speaking adults in San Francisco since 1983. Project READ is a member of the California Literacy Campaign, a statewide project of more than 100 public libraries initiated and supported by the California State Library. Since its inception, Project READ has served more than 4,000 adults seeking to improve their reading and writing skills. A snapshot of our clientele shows that 64 percent are African American, 27 percent are unemployed, 90 percent are reading below a fifth-grade level, and 85 percent are between the ages of 35 and 60.

Like other library-based literacy programs and many adult education facilities, Project READ has sought to enhance its basic literacy instruction by developing a Computer Learning Lab. As adult educators, we understand that basic computer comfort issues need to be addressed, as they must with any first-time computer user. We also realize that to be most effective, instructional software must be fully integrated into the curriculum. Because we are a volunteer-based program, we know that the tutors have to buy into the concept of computer-assisted instruction for the computer lab to be a success. Unfortunately, the wide variety of instructional software available and the growing excitement of the Internet can sometimes contribute to an "if we build it, they will come" mentality. As literacy practitioners, I believe that our basic challenge will always be to make the computer lab a comfortable, non-intimidating, and exciting environment for learning.

The Computer Lab

At Project READ, our computer lab coordinator, Brian Castagne, has been very successful in helping to increase the use of the computer lab by learners and tutors. His basic philosophy is to make the computers themselves as transparent as possible. Adult learners should first and foremost have a positive experience when working in the computer lab, in order to find the information they seek, learn the skills they need, and not be frustrated by the technology. We are, after all, working in a learner-centered program and the computer lab should conform to this basic premise that guides what we do.

Each adult learner is asked to spend three to six hours, depending on his or her previous computer experience, in computer lab introductory classes. These classes are designed to help learners increase their computer skills and computer comfort while they are engaged in project-based activities. During this time, Brian gives the learners an overview of the equipment without being too technical. The learners begin by working with some simple learning software (Spell-It Deluxe) to help them become comfortable using a mouse and keyboard. They enjoy the game-like qualities of the software and also appreciate the spelling skills that are being developed at the same time. The learners are encouraged to sign up for a free e-mail account with Hotmail or Yahoo. Brian takes them through the steps of establishing a user name and password, and soon they are communicating with Project READ staff, other learners, and their own tutors. Later in the introductory sessions, the learners work on other popular programs (Type to Learn and Ultimate Phonics) and learn how to search for information on the Internet. Adult learners also receive an introduction to the Project READ website (http://www.ProjectReadSF. org). On this site, they can find links for e-mail, electronic greetings, Internet search engines, as well as electronic versions of *Update*, the Project READ newsletter, containing the writings of many other adult learners.

After completion, each learner is awarded a Computer Lab License that enables him or her to use the lab at any time and to take part in any other computer workshops being offered. We encourage use of the lab by tutor/learner teams as a regular part of their instruction. In some ways, it has been a greater challenge to encourage the volunteer tutors to make use of the lab than it has been to involve the adult learners. The majority of Project READ's volunteer tutors are young professionals who spend their days at work at the computer screen. It is not surprising that they might not jump at the chance to do so again in the evening during their tutoring session. The staff at Project READ attempt to make them understand that their adult learners do not have this regular access to the personal computer. For the learner, the computer can be new and exciting and it is a powerful tool in their overall plan of instruction.

When I first joined the Project READ team as director in 1999, the lab seemed to be deserted most of the time. Now, when the tutor/learner team enters the lab during evening hours, they are likely to find a lively and exciting atmosphere filled with communication and interaction. Each computer station is in use, the chocolate candies are floating about, and a true community of learners/computer users is being forged.

Free Computers

Project READ has also instituted a computer-donation program that provides adult learners with free computer systems for the home. Through an article in our newsletter, we asked individuals and businesses to donate their old computers. We were astonished by the results and soon found ourselves inundated with personal computers of all shapes, sizes, and operating systems. With the help of some volunteer computer technicians, we were able to clean up and prepare eight personal computers that were then offered to Project READ learners through a raffle. Each PC had a CD drive and was loaded with free Internet and basic instructional software. The first lucky winner was a learner with four school-age children, who could not have afforded to buy a home computer. Her children were literally jumping up and down with excitement when their mother's name was drawn as the winner.

WHAT WE DO

The staff of Project READ are committed to making the Computer Learning Lab a useful and well-utilized component of our adult literacy instruction. We have found that as adult learners become more comfortable with using the computers in the lab, they also become more adventurous in seeking out information on the Internet and more confident and successful when working with educational software. Not only does computer technology become an important component of literacy instruction but computers also become a tool for lifelong learning.

Here is a sample of tasks and projects that have been performed by learners in the computer lab.

When faced with a move, a learner used the Internet to research available housing, obtain quotes from movers, and use Mapquest to pinpoint locations.

Another learner sent e-mail messages to local politicians in support of legislation to expand adult literacy services.

A message of sympathy was sent to the Kennedy family after the death of John Kennedy Jr.

A learner wrote a story based on childhood memories and illustrated the story with a photo after he learned to use the scanner.

A learner located the Internet address of his hometown paper in Houston, Texas, and began reading this newspaper online.

■ 19 ■

Public Library Literacy Programs

A Blueprint for the Future

MARTÍN GÓMEZ

My goal here is to outline a possible future blueprint for public library–based literacy programs. You might wonder what qualifies me to speak on this topic. I'm wondering too! I am not a literacy expert. But I have spent the last 23 years of my professional life working in public libraries in San Diego, Oakland, and at one time in Chicago, my home town. For the past four years I've served as the executive director of the Brooklyn Public Library in New York City.

During my career I've had the opportunity to work closely with Gary Strong (see chapter 14) and Al Bennett as a member of the library development team that implemented the California Literacy Campaign. As director of the Oakland Public Library, I had the pleasure of working with Leslie McGinnis (see chapter 3) and Norma Jones, supporting their efforts to develop the Second Start Literacy Program. And today, I am pleased to be working with Susan O'Connor (see chapter 16), director of literacy services for the Brooklyn Public Library, shaping programs for students enrolled in our literacy programs.

A Look at the 1980s

But for me, the last half of the 1980s will always serve as a benchmark in the public library–based literacy movement. In 1984 the California State

Based on a speech given at the Libraries and Literacy: Partnerships and Perspectives Conference, Chicago, Illinois, September 9, 1999.

Library launched a statewide literacy initiative. It was an incredibly exciting time for me professionally. Within a two-year period, 48 public libraries were granted LSCA dollars to establish literacy instruction programs. Within four years, the California State legislature passed the California Literacy Act, providing a consistent source of funding for public library literacy efforts.

That experience has shaped my perspective about public library–based literacy programs. And it has given me some insight regarding what public libraries and librarians might do to make a greater contribution to improve literacy in the United States.

Preparing for this presentation has been a journey for me in more ways than one. As a result of my journey, I've come to the following conclusion. Every couple of years all public library directors should be required to give a presentation on public library–based literacy programs. This act alone would force us to take inventory of what we do and don't know about the subject and perhaps even feel a bit guilty about the need to be more supportive of such an important social issue.

I have no doubt that the public library–based literacy movement has grown and matured since my days at the California State Library. But since that time I've seen the need for adult literacy services outpace the growth of our collective effort. At the very least, the movement within public libraries has held ground. But we are still swimming upstream and the current is getting stronger.

Recent national statistics indicate that roughly one out of five adults in the United States are still in need of basic literacy assistance. According to the National Adult Literacy Survey, 21 to 23 percent of the adult U.S. population (or between 40 to 44 million) displayed difficulty using certain reading, writing, and computational skills considered necessary for functioning in everyday life.

Definitions of Literacy

The importance and necessity of being "functionally literate" have grown significantly due, in great part, to the explosion of information technology. The ability to have access to and competency in using technology has become a fundamental requirement in today's labor market. This has created a de facto demand for enhanced literacy skills. And without a solid foundation of basic reading and writing skills, opportunities for meaningful employment are severely limited.

To add confusion to the issue, the word "literacy" has been attached to so many issues that the focus on the basic literacy needs of our adult population has gotten lost in sound bites like "cultural literacy," "computer literacy," and "financial literacy." I'm talking about public library programs that enhance one's ability to read and write. Or, as defined by the National Adult Literacy Survey of 1993," using printed and written information to function in society, to achieve one's goals, and develop one's knowledge and potential."

As I set out on my journey, I wanted to know what has happened to the public library–based literacy movement over the past ten years, not just in California but nationally. How have public libraries shaped national policy and how has that policy shaped the role and nature of the public library–based adult literacy landscape? But most importantly, I wanted to know if we've made a difference.

Unfortunately, I didn't find the answers to the questions that I posed. But I did identify a handful of critical milestones that have, in theory, contributed to the movement. My conclusion, with some exceptions, is that even with these major milestones we, the public library community, have not done enough to enhance our commitment to literacy. Here's what I found.

In 1988 the University of Wisconsin at Madison produced *Libraries and Literacy Education,* a seminal report by Douglas Zweizig, Jane Robbins, and others. This report, which surveyed hundreds of public libraries in the nation, developed key definitions regarding the various types of literacy efforts by libraries, identified the important roles that libraries play in providing literacy education, and pinpointed the importance of library management's attitude toward literacy efforts.

About the same time, the American Library Association established the National Coalition for Literacy, a group of nonprofit organizations and literacy service providers. The purpose of the coalition is to be the "authoritative commentator on emerging literacy issues and works to expand public awareness, foster collaboration, provide communication, encourage applied research, and provide a leadership voice for the literacy movement."

In 1991 the National Institute for Literacy was created to "be the hub of national literacy efforts. By serving as a resource for the literacy community, the Institute assists in addressing urgent national priorities, upgrading the workforce, reducing welfare dependency, raising the standard of living and creating safer communities."

One of its responsibilities is to "assist in uniting the national effort to reach National Education Goal 5 for adult literacy and lifelong learning.

Goal 5 states that "by the year 2000 every adult American will be literate and will possess the knowledge and skill necessary to compete in a global economy and exercise the rights and responsibilities of citizenship."

In 1993 the National Adult Literacy survey was completed. The survey established the first comprehensive, statistically reliable source of data on literacy in the United States, and established three literacy "scales"—prose, document, and quantitative literacy—each scale reflecting a different type of real-life literacy task. But, more importantly, the survey gave us a common language by which to measure individual literacy levels.

Recently, the Lila Wallace-Reader's Digest Fund invested more than $4 million in 13 public libraries to support a series of innovative literacy instruction methods that will, we hope, result in the identification of strategies that not only work but can be replicated by other public library–based literacy service providers. Literacy in Libraries across America was designed by ALA in concert with the Lila Wallace-Reader's Digest Fund to "coordinate technical assistance to the 13 participating libraries and to provide leadership, services to the field."

Work in the 1990s

In 1998 the Workforce Investment Act was signed into law and has the potential to have a major impact on the adult literacy movement. Public libraries need to be ready with proposals for creative projects that can demonstrate how our adult literacy programs will help under- and unemployed populations make the transition from welfare to work.

Also in 1998, the Reading Excellence Act became law. Hundreds of millions of dollars are available as competitive grants to states to improve reading skills of students and the instructional practices of teachers. The act also expands family literacy programs and early childhood intervention programs. Again, public libraries need to be ready with proposals for creative projects that can demonstrate how we can help schools, teachers, and other qualified agencies to develop creative early intervention literacy programs for students and their families.

In 1998 ALA's executive board voted to provide funds for enhancements to the Office for Literacy and Outreach Services (OLOS) to enhance the association's ability to provide effective leadership for library-based literacy efforts. And in April 1999, National Literacy Forum published a five-page set of recommendations calling for expanded public support for literacy, improvements to teaching quality for literacy instruction, and strengthening the role of libraries in providing and supporting literacy services, to name just a few.

As public libraries, how have we benefited from these policy initiatives? How have they helped shape our programs and enabled us to improve services in our communities?

> Public libraries have generated increased visibility regarding the issue of literacy, efforts aimed at improving literacy, and the need for action in our communities.
>
> New national, state, and local partnerships have been established.
>
> In some cases, these initiatives have resulted in enhanced funding opportunities.

In many instances, public libraries have gained a place at the national policy table. And locally, many public libraries are leading the public policy debate on literacy.

How have our programs benefited from these efforts?

> Public library–based literacy programs have expanded from one-on-one instructional methods to group and small classroom oriented techniques.
>
> By having educators involved in the design of our programs, we have learned more about the process of learning or how people learn.
>
> In addition, we have learned that a learner-centered curriculum is a more effective one.
>
> And we are beginning to learn that we have to be more accountable to internal stakeholders
>
> We have also learned that successful programs are ones that are more fully integrated into traditional library services.

But with all of this "learning" we are still swimming upstream. For all of our effort, for all of our achievements, public libraries have not fully exploited their role as literacy-centered institutions. I know that there are some notable exceptions to what I've just said, but overall, we, the public library community, have not risen to the challenge. We have not assumed our share of responsibility for improving literacy levels in this country.

Perhaps our slow organizational response to literacy efforts is a reflection of the challenge that public libraries have assumed in relation to information technology. This is not a bad thing, simply a reflection of the leadership within the public library movement and the critical need that we've had to position our institution as the public provider of information technology at this moment in time. I might add that Bill Gates has had something to do with this.

Every librarian can tell you that as a result of computer technology and the Internet, the nature of library work has changed more than any of us could have imagined ten years ago. Technology is changing the public library. But then, maybe this is just an excuse?

I don't think it's too late for public libraries to assume greater responsibility and I'd like to offer some suggestions about how we might do just that and what we might consider.

1. Public libraries could reposition their mission statements to reflect a greater responsibility for creating a literate population. As staff from ALA said in their report to the executive board, "librarians must claim literacy as a central issue and a professional value."

2. Strong mission statements are policy positions that can lead to plans of action.

3. We could adopt a 10 percent solution. Public libraries could pledge to commit ten percent of their resources to improving literacy services within their respective communities by the year 2009, a significant challenge to be sure, but the impact of such a shift would be felt throughout the country. And if an organization like ALA joined in this effort—need I say more?

4. This would mean that libraries would most likely have to begin to shift resources away from "traditional" library programs. Our staff and patrons would need to be convinced about the larger social value of this effort, not as a reduction in other services.

5. We need to get more political. I mean this in the best and worst definitions of the word. We should identify and support candidates that support our literacy agenda. We need to support them financially and volunteer on behalf of their campaigns. What elected officials are we cultivating locally, in the statehouse, or on capitol hill? This is incredibly important. Letter-writing campaigns are important but we must also develop and execute a well-crafted legislative strategy that includes all of our partners. And, when necessary, we should include public demonstrations. We did it with technology (LSTA, eRate). Why can't we do it with literacy?

6. We must make a commitment to further institutionalize literacy efforts in our libraries. This means holding other library departments responsible for making commitments to support the literacy office. It means creating opportunities for library staff to meet students and tutors, to participate (on work time) in the program either as students or tutors.

7. We would need to find ways to strengthen or introduce (or in some cases, reintroduce) literacy service to inmates in our communities.

8. It's time to "legitimize" literacy instruction as a discipline that requires support from institutions of higher learning, including graduate library schools.

9. We would have to ask our librarians to become educators and, in some respects, ask our teachers to become librarians. We might even have to ask our literacy program staff to become certified literacy instructors. And we should support the development of a credential program in literacy instruction for librarians and teachers

10. We must develop coalitions with labor. Public libraries are in a strategically advantageous position to develop literacy programs that complement welfare-to-work programs currently being funded at the federal level. And our experience with technology makes this an even more attractive proposition.

11. It's time to begin providing instructional services to preschoolers and elementary kids who are at risk, establishing public library–based early intervention programs, much in the same way we did for adults in California and other parts of the country in the 1980s.

12. Children's service programs can easily begin to develop early intervention programs with Head Start and elementary schools; early reading intervention initiatives are not only politically attractive to elected officials but there is a generation of children out there who need our help.

13. We must get the welfare mentality out of literacy. Let's continue on framing literacy as an economic issue that will help build productive communities.

And, as former Senator Paul Simon said, public library directors need to assume greater leadership on behalf of literacy in our communities. Are there any takers?

Leadership does make a difference. As shown in Table 5, Level of Literacy Activity is positively associated with values of key "leadership" variables, including: priority given to literacy by the library director and library board; amount of money spent annually on literacy activities; attention administrators give to literacy compared to other library programs; and centrality of literacy to the library's mission in the view of library administrators, board, and staff. *Survey,* p. 24

▪ 20 ▪

The American Library Association's Literacy Initiatives

History and Hope

PEGGY BARBER

Libraries, librarians, and the American Library Association have been involved in literacy services since the earliest days of public libraries and the 1876 launch of the association. Most of this good work has gone unnoticed by everyone, including the library profession and ALA. A quick review of this history documents opportunities lost, but also suggests progress and hope: hope for the continued growth of excellent literacy programs in all types of libraries; hope that librarians will embrace the issue and seize the power, satisfaction, and recognition for providing a vital and valuable service.

As early as the end of the nineteenth century librarians at ALA conferences were debating the appropriate role for libraries in teaching adults to read. The debate focused on "Americanization" of new immigrants. Should they be taught English, or should libraries collect books in foreign languages? Should librarians teach?

In 1916 at the ALA conference in Asbury Park, New Jersey, John Foster Carr, Immigration Publication Society director said that he found remarkable all the profession had accomplished in teaching literacy. Carr said his organization knew of more than 500 libraries with programs for the foreign born. "The sad part," he said, "was that librarians had achieved their accomplishments so quietly that the public was unaware how great an effort they had expended, how dedicated they were, or how much success they had realized."[1] Carr said his organization knew of more than 500 libraries with programs for the foreign born.

In more recent history, literacy has remained a "behind the scenes" issue. In 1968 ALA established the Coordinating Committee on Library Service to the Disadvantaged and founded an Office for Library Service to the Disadvantaged and Unserved. Both quietly incorporated the issue of literacy. In 1975 ALA received a Department of Education grant for a literacy program that resulted in the publication of Helen Lyman's manual, *Literacy and the Nation's Libraries*. The Office for Service to the Disadvantaged eventually became the Office for Library Outreach Services, and in 1995 its name was finally changed to the Office for *Literacy* and Outreach Services (OLOS) (emphasis is mine).

In 1981 ALA founded the National Coalition for Literacy, the organization sponsoring the Ad Council literacy campaign, which brought the problem of adult functional illiteracy to the attention of the American public. The initial campaign included establishment of the Contact Literacy Center, a national 800 number for tutors and learners and a database of literacy programs across the nation. It also inspired other public-awareness efforts such as Project Literacy U.S. (PLUS)—the unprecedented ABC/PBS collaboration that included prime-time specials, abundant public-service announcements, and community outreach. Former First Lady Barbara Bush made literacy her issue. There were prime-time National Literacy Honors specials broadcast from the White House. ALA remained involved—but not out in front. Today, ALA continues to provide staff support to the National Coalition for Literacy, and serves as its fiscal agent.

Grant Support in the 1990s

In the early 1990s, with funding from the Bell Atlantic Foundation, Cargill Inc., and the Viburnum Foundation, ALA—and OLOS—led the development of family literacy programs in public libraries. With this grant support, ALA provided libraries with funds, training, model programs, materials, and technical assistance. These programs built on the strong tradition of children's services in libraries, helping parents and children to learn to read and enjoy reading and literacy activities to break the cycle of illiteracy. At about this time, the Association for Library Service to Children (ALSC) received a grant from the Prudential Foundation for a program called Born to Read, which involved demonstration projects between health-care providers and librarians to reach at-risk parents-to-be. Born to Read is still going strong, as are family literacy programs in many libraries.

There are literacy preconferences, programs, and meetings of the Literacy Assembly at ALA conferences. The Public Library Association gives an annual award to recognize outstanding library literacy efforts. ALA Graphics produces beautiful posters and other promotional materials to promote reading, libraries, and literacy. Since the mid-1990s, the Association for Specialized and Cooperative Library Agencies has directed Roads to Learning, a public libraries and learning disabilities initiative funded by the Emily Hall Tremaine Foundation.

In 1995 ALA's literacy efforts received a major boost when the Lila Wallace-Reader's Digest Fund approached ALA to lead a three-year, $4 million national initiative to strengthen library-based adult literacy programs. The project, Literacy in Libraries Across America (LILAA), provided funding to 13 of the best existing literacy programs in public libraries and developed a powerful leadership cadre that is changing the library literacy scene. When the initial project ended, ALA funded a literacy officer position beginning in 1999.

Also in 1995, ALA joined the Library of Congress Center for the Book, National Institute for Literacy, and a private donor named Harold McGraw to support a study of library-based adult literacy programs. Its purpose was to refocus attention on the important institutional and service roles of libraries in literacy. Released in 1996, the report by Gail Spangenberg was titled "Even Anchors Need Lifelines." Spangenberg said, "Judging by . . . the large number of public libraries now involved in the provision of adult literacy service (some 7,000 not counting branches), public libraries also embrace literacy as a central part of their ongoing mission, although with occasional ambivalence. They are a community anchor for literacy—or as one project advisor put it, they could well be seen as the 'irreducible backbone of the literacy movement.'"[2] Spangenberg's report made much of the discontinuance of LSCA Title VI, which had provided direct federal support for library literacy programs. One of the major "lifelines" is gone.

Most library literacy programs are still launched with grant funds, while librarians tend to apply for grants that say "library" in their title and are reasonably accessible. Federal funds for literacy and English-as-a-second-language training are now distributed primarily through block grants to the states. Although libraries are mentioned in the legislation, the testing and reporting requirements put federal funding out of reach for most public library literacy programs. Libraries traditionally serve the lowest level of adult new readers. They could use targeted federal, state, and local support. Unfortunately, support for literacy programs has not been a priority on ALA's legislative agenda.

The valuable role of library literacy programs was recognized in 1995, when ALA was honored with a Leadership Award from Literacy Volunteers of America (LVA) for "its profound influence over and enduring support of the literacy movement." According to the citation, "ALA has encouraged libraries to provide direct support to community literacy programs, through funding, space, staff and materials for tutors and students. It has added expertise and a strong voice to the literacy field's effort to secure supportive public policies and funding for adult basic education. And perhaps most meaningful of all, ALA has sustained the fight for intellectual freedom and access to information for all, regardless of race, religion, age, national origin, social or political views, or the ability to read or speak English with fluency." The LVA award to ALA seemed designed to encourage more leadership. Unfortunately, it was hardly noticed.

Also in 1995 ALA adopted Goal 2000, a five-year initiative to position the association and libraries for the twenty-first century. While it stressed the importance of connecting libraries to digital information networks, Goal 2000 focused on human services rather than technology. It said "The American Library Association must be as closely associated with the idea of the public's right to a free and open information society—intellectual participation—as it is with the idea of intellectual freedom." Clearly the ability to read is the most basic step toward intellectual participation. Literacy was apparently a key element of ALA's national agenda, but it wasn't mentioned in the Goal 2000 plan.

Literacy on the Front Burner

Progress came in 1998 when ALA adopted five key action areas. Literacy is one of the five! Those key action priorities—diversity, education and continuous learning, equity of access, intellectual freedom, and twenty-first-century literacy—are now moving ALA's latest strategic plan, ALAction 2005. Literacy has hit the front burner. Is the fire hot? Not quite, but again there is hope.

Here are some of the reasons for hope. ALA is funding a literacy officer position. There is sustained leadership from the literacy officer and a dedicated member group—inspired and led by many of the LILAA project directors and staff. A growing e-mail list provides substantive discussion on library literacy issues. ALA and library literacy leaders were included—and were a strong voice—in the Literacy Summit organized in February 2000 by the National Institute for Literacy. Funders such as the Lila Wallace-Reader's Digest Fund continue to recognize, support—and document with new research—the library role in literacy. There are new funders supporting library literacy programs, such as the Verizon (formerly GTE) Foundation. Literacy programs are reaching across the association. For example, ALA's Public Programs Office now has two projects funded by the National Endowment for the Humanities: National Connections and Prime Time Family Literacy provide reading and discussion programs for adult new readers and their families. A new ALA Standing Committee on Literacy was approved during the association's 2000 Annual Conference in Chicago. The school and academic librarians are leading information literacy movements. Soon the whole profession will understand that we will teach or be irrelevant.

So why has literacy been so marginal an issue in the American Library Association? Why hasn't an ALA president ever made literacy the association's focus? Why didn't our profession see what state librarian Gary Strong (now in New York City's Queens, see chapter 14) did in California? Strong invested big chunks of LSCA funding in library literacy, which inspired the state legislature to invest more than $50 million in state funds for literacy and family literacy programs in public libraries. There are currently ongoing literacy programs in more than 150 public libraries in California. Thousands of adults have learned to read. Thousands of parents and children have found new opportunities.

Librarians and ALA stand tall for intellectual freedom issues. Why not literacy? ALA has a Freedom to Read Foundation. Do we really mean it? It's perhaps easier for us to embrace an intellectual concept such as the First Amendment, than to teach reading to adults and families who need a second chance. I'm not suggesting that we replace one professional value with another. I am suggesting that we increase our power by increasing our passion. A literate pubic demands good libraries; good libraries create a literate public. It makes sense.

NOTES

1. Deanna B. Marcum and Elizabeth W. Stone, "Literacy: The Library Legacy," *American Libraries* (March 1991): 202–5.

2. Gail Spangenberg, *Even Anchors Need Lifelines* (Washington, D.C.: Center for the Book in the Library of Congress, 1996), p. 116.

▪ 21 ▪

Bridging the Information Chasm

ALA's Office for Literacy and Outreach Services

SATIA MARSHALL ORANGE

Libraries "ensure access to information for all."[1] The message of the American Library Association (ALA), in a society where access to information is the key to survival, is that libraries must respond to the information needs of *everyone* in their communities. The sustainability of these communities is dependent on information; their information vehicles must be comfortably and equitably accessible. Libraries can and must ensure that. It is true, however, that the equitable library service mandated by ALA is not always available for *everyone* in *every* library community in the United States.

Thus, the mission statement recently revised by the Advisory Committee of the Association's Office for Literacy and Outreach Services (OLOS) extends ALA's message with these special emphases:

> OLOS serves the Association by supporting and promoting literacy and equity of information access initiatives for traditionally underserved populations. These populations include new and non-readers, people geographically isolated, people with disabilities, rural and urban poor people, and people discriminated against based on race, ethnicity, sexual orientation, age, language and social class.[2]

The placement of "new and non-readers" as the first population indicated in the OLOS mission statement above is no accident. This unanimous decision by advisory committee members validates the recommendations of a comprehensive review of the office in 1997. It also

159

acknowledges the reality that the survival of many of the other groups included in the statement is too often complicated by their limited reading skills, for whatever reason; for example, English as a second language, limited formal education, disabilities, complications of poverty, hunger, and homelessness, etc.

Adult literacy initiatives have been a focus of OLOS for most of its existence, even when the office's target service population was described as librarians serving the "disadvantaged." An updated mission statement was set in place to more clearly and dramatically address the need for effective library services to traditionally underserved populations. The office's efforts today target library directors and administrators, trustees, and those library staff members who conceive, plan, and provide frontline delivery of information services, collections, and programs in local library communities.

Information Chasm Rather Than Digital Divide

As the information challenges of the twenty-first century become more apparent, there are ever-increasing discussions about the digital divide. A recent exchange on an OLOS electronic discussion list highlighted the limited focus of this phrase. The list subscribers sought to identify an expressive term to describe the issue more adequately.

Conversations among researchers, politicians, practitioners, and non-profit organizations send messages translated by news media about the "haves and have nots," and their conflicting levels of familiarity with the new technology. These terms are legitimate in statement and purpose, and are validated by the numbers of high school dropouts and unemployed workers, along with the more stringent requirements for today's employment positions. However, even the use of "divide" with "digital" expresses too succinct a meaning to accurately reflect the impact on adult learner issues and those of other OLOS mission placeholders. I suggest that the term "divide" is more of a problematic description than even the term "gap."

An alternative term to consider is "chasm" rather than "divide." A chasm is more dramatic than "gap," and it suggests the need for extreme but credible (even architecturally exact) possibilities. Strategically designed efforts must be considered to bridge the great expanse between those familiar with the array of vehicles for accessing information and those less comfortable, if at all aware of information access alternatives. Considering the space between the two groups as approachable rather than divided also conveys the message that it can be strengthened with data, training, opportunities, and hope that could fill it, or at least lessen its dimensions and its defeating impact. "Divide," on the other hand, implies the need for battling a wall or a division, a negative reference between those comfortable and well acquainted with the new vehicles for information retrieval and those who are not. The difference, I admit, is purely attitudinal.

The Challenge

The challenge for ALA, OLOS, and you, their members, internal and external partners in supporting those for whom this information phenomenon directly impacts, is to bridge this "chasm" with opportunities for encouragement, collaboration, training, and support. The development of effective information-delivery systems purposefully designed, in part, by the people for whom they are targeted, is in many formats already in place, or at least being researched and designed in local communities, as well as on many organizations' national agendas.

Libraries of all kinds are and can continue to be the catalysts that advocate the use of adult learning systems, whether in university and community colleges, nonprofit adult literacy organizations and agencies, schools and corporations, or in the libraries themselves. Libraries, by their acceptance of municipally assigned civic responsibilities, can become more identified as one of the champions in their communities for nurturing and fine-tuning their policies and practices to eliminate the information "chasms" in their own institutions. These championship honors can be shared with others in their communities who are successfully addressing similar issues. The "community championship circle" should be flexible enough to allow for increasing involvement; the more champions, the more sustainable the communities.

And finally, OLOS encourages libraries to use similar energies and their collective expertise to share the adult learner services with other traditionally underserved populations in their communities who are faced with multiple service challenges. The experience in OLOS has suggested that although the objectives and strategies are similar, other populations' service needs do overlap.

OLOS Support of Adult Literacy

At its last Midwinter Meeting of the twentieth century, the Executive Board of the American Library Association approved a most significant recommendation. It prioritized adult literacy in libraries by adding a literacy officer position to the Office for Literacy and Outreach Services. And the benefits to the profession of that one appointment continue to reverberate throughout the association. ALA's achievements in garnering and solidifying external partnerships cannot be overstated. Dale Phillips Lipschultz admirably accepted the challenge and nobly and successfully administered the objectives.

The vision for the Office for Literacy and Outreach Services mandates the delivery of information services to librarians and their communities to effectively encourage and support adult literacy in their institutions. OLOS resources will allow them to make informed decisions about how to impact new and nonreading adults and families in their libraries, whether as mainstays in library infrastructures, as project initiatives, or as ongoing support of community adult literacy agencies. Throughout the association, OLOS's goal is to support libraries as they participate, on any level, on behalf of the adult literacy community, and with other service communities as well.

Thanks to the collaborative efforts of ALA and the Lila Wallace-Reader's Digest Fund Initiative—Literacy in Libraries Across America (LILAA)—the office has developed a strong strategic plan with an effective path toward improved services to librarians addressing adult learners. Because of their continuing successful outcomes, these strategies now serve as models for "bridging the chasm" for other OLOS mission populations as well.

The OLOS strategic planning objectives parallel those of its literacy component. The variations can be found in their focus, however. The OLOS adult literacy component may be easier to understand because of its definition, its current prominence in the public eye, and the recent availability of significant funding. The other OLOS components cover other outreach populations, all of whom may be directly affected by the constraints of limited literacy skills. Future program initiatives will broaden the service strategies to combine both components for successful outcomes.

Vision for the Future

OLOS is a small, non-revenue-generating office with a large responsibility within ALA, which, with the support of its advisory committee, ALA administrative staff, and the Executive Board, has a clear vision for the future that involves teaming with internal and external partners and service recipients. The major thrust for cooperation with other units within the association and national partners who target the populations identified in the mission statement requires the appreciation and respect of multiple perspectives and the sharing of resources. Therefore, the visions for the office are to:

broaden the "consumer" base of collaborators within the association and the profession, and better address their library-focused needs through its various networks of outreach library staff;

more aggressively encourage internal (and external) partnering of association staff development initiatives, including coauthoring publications, participating in inter-unit informational initiatives on effective techniques for addressing the "information chasm," and gleaning information from other units' leadership and approaches for successful outcomes;

work with the ALA Public Information Office and the Publishing Department to bolster campaigns on library services to new and nonreaders as well as other populations, while supporting the collaborative efforts of libraries with their local partner organizations on local and national levels;

work closely with ALA's Diversity Office, the Office for Human Resource Development and Recruitment (HRDR), and other ALA units to ensure collaborative support for libraries that reflects diversity in planning, execution, and participation. The diversity officer also coordinates the ALA Spectrum Initiatives, which facilitates the recruitment of people of color with financial support for library school attendance;[3]

support ongoing dialogue and action planning with the proposed ALA Council Committee on Literacy, utilizing the combined expertise of its representative members from ALA's member divisions and roundtables;[4]

link to the Internet websites of other ALA units, affiliates, and partners for shared access to resources that support adult literacy throughout the library and adult literacy communities;

keep the association leadership—i.e., Executive Board, Council, division presidents, roundtable chairs, membership, and ALA partners—appraised of new efforts, initiatives, outcomes, strategies, and

> opportunities for support and involvement in adult literacy and
> other outreach initiatives;
>
> cooperate with the ALA Washington and Development Offices to
> include adult learner issues in legislation and funding approaches
> for other outreach groups;
>
> disseminate information about the Building Literacy Coalitions Initia-
> tive, recently funded by Verizon, and other adult literacy initiatives
> to other library outreach networks for the benefit and awareness of
> their local library users;
>
> encourage emphasis on adult learners with OLOS liaison groups, espe-
> cially the national associations of librarians of color, as they consider
> initiatives for their local service communities;[5]
>
> And, finally, advocate for more contemporary curriculum emphasis in
> library schools that comprehensively address library outreach issues
> and service strategies for new professionals.

Can We Achieve Our Vision?

A recent publication entitled *Toward an Information Bill of Rights and Responsibilities* introduces a Bill of Information Rights that enunciates the rights of governments, individuals, and corporate citizens to information.[6] One of the authors, Jorge Reina Schement, suggests the crucial right to information as one of universal access for all individuals.

The concept of ensuring practical access for all to a ramp onto the emerging electronic hierarchy of information presents a profoundly frightening picture for OLOS mission populations. The dangers exist in the inequities of access that truly separate our society. That "ramp" will not serve the majority of OLOS populations because they will not see the ramp, and will be unable to navigate through the information society promised in this millennium. They will not only be left behind, they will be ignored. Therein is the concern for equity as an ALA key action area versus equality, as expressed in the First Amendment of the Bill of Rights.

Targeting ALA's internal organization and external partners is certainly a challenge, but one hampered by tradition and practice, and not by pos-sibilities. Some public librarians feel strongly that they are already effec-tively addressing traditionally underserved populations. Closer review reveals, however, that too few unit contingencies within the membership divisions and roundtables focus their energies on the "information chasm." Their interests and willingness to collaborate for more effective treatment and services for OLOS-designated populations have been stated, however, even by their leadership. Therefore, accomplishing a professionwide approach to filling the "chasm" with effective data is strongly within the realm of probability.

So there is a positive answer to what is accomplishable. Here are some examples of accomplishments already in place:

OLOS has designated funds for working with other ALA units on web-based continuing education, staff development on adult literacy and other mission populations.

The Public Library Association (PLA), a division of ALA, has included consideration for basic literacy in its recently published *Planning for Results: A Public Library Transformation Process.*[7]

The OLOS website at http://www.ala.org/olos includes resources on library services to all of the traditionally underserved populations that can be accessed by libraries via the Internet.

The first Jean E. Coleman Library Outreach Lecture was also inaugurated at the 2000 ALA Annual Conference. The first lecture, presented by ALA Past-President Barbara J. Ford (1998–1999), focused on the global approach to library outreach services, and identified the importance of including adult literacy in libraries. The second lecture, for the 2001 Annual Conference in San Francisco, will focus on adult literacy and its impact on the literacy field and library populations.

Sarah Ann Long, ALA Past-President (1999–2000), introduced the presidential theme for the 2000 Annual Conference in Chicago, as "Libraries Build Sustainable Communities." A number of programs before and during that conference, and in a separately published brochure, suggested alternatives for many in libraries who are not only traditionally underserved but also underrepresented, to participate in their communities' decisions. Long's invitation to "consider making your library the heart of the community decisions, especially those regarding the three Es of sustainability: environment, economics, and equity," provides an intriguing opportunity for libraries to increase the community participation of their users. Just think! Adult learners in libraries will have the immediate opportunity to participate in negotiating their communities' futures.[8]

ALA's Office for Literacy and Outreach Services can make the difference in addressing the needs of adult learners and others in library communities. Communities must be enlarged to include all the involved, especially the adult learners themselves. The American Library Association will be the resource that supports libraries and library staff for effective delivery of services to this important population. We've turned the corner and we see the bright possibilities with our internal and external partners. We can make it happen. Join us!

NOTES

1. The mission of the American Library Association can be found at http://www.ala.org.

2. Adopted by the OLOS Advisory Committee, June 1999.

3. The Spectrum Scholarship Initiative can have a great impact on the effectiveness of some literacy initiatives, since literacy professionals of color are limited in number.

4. OLOS will be the ALA staff liaison for this committee to be established by the summer of 2001; the formation of the ALA Council Committee on Literacy was presented as a resolution at the 2000 ALA Annual Conference and is awaiting final authorization by ALA's Committee on Committees for final acceptance by the ALA Council. (Passed at Annual Conference, 2000.)

5. American Indian Library Association (AILA), Asian Pacific American Librarian Association (APALA), Black Caucus of the American Library Association (BCALA), Chinese American Librarians Association (CALA), REFORMA: National Association to Promote Library and Information Services to Latinos and the Spanish Speaking.

6. *Toward an Information Bill of Rights and Responsibilities,* ed. by Charles M. Firestone and Jorge Reina Schement (Washington, D.C.: Aspen Institute, 1995).

7. *Planning for Results: A Public Library Transformation Process* (Chicago and London: American Library Association, 1999).

8. Message from ALA President Sarah Ann Long, "Libraries Can Help Build Sustainable Communities," *American Libraries* 31 (June/July 2000): 7.

▪ 22 ▪
Coda: Word

GRACEANNE A. DE CANDIDO

On more than one occasion my family and I have trekked to Jonesborough, Tennessee, for the National Storytelling Festival sponsored by NAPPS, the National Association for the Preservation and Perpetuation of Storytelling (now the National Storytelling Center). These are times full of marvels, where professional tellers, librarians, preachers, schoolteachers, family historians, and people who just love a good yarn gather to listen, to tell, and to share.

During one of these trips, I was waiting my turn at the outhouse and began to chat with the woman in front of me, who turned out to be a librarian. She told me that she was in charge of the literacy volunteers in her library. One of the techniques they used was to transcribe on the library computer the family and cultural stories their students told, and use those stories as reading texts. The people learning to read were delighted to see their own words in print, different cultures and ideas were shared among the students, and the problem of textbooks was solved. I was enchanted by this: oral history, multiculturalism, grassroots use of computer technology, literacy, and the power of the word all woven together into one basic and useful basket.

Originally published in the "Brazen Overtures" editorial column of *Wilson Library Bulletin*, February 1994, p. 6. Reproduced by special permission of the H. W. Wilson Co., New York.

There was a time when I believed, along with many of my colleagues, that libraries had enough to handle without tackling the enormous problem of illiteracy. Two things changed my mind.

The first was an interview I conducted with Senator Paul Simon (D–Ill., now retired). Simon described the shame and fear of many illiterate adults. He said, though, that going to the public library for help did not have the stigma attached to it that going to a school or other public center might have. People feel a sense of ownership in their libraries; there is no shame in asking questions there.

The other thing that changed my mind was the development of libraries in the past decade. Traditionally the home of ideas that dwell in books, libraries have become the place for ideas on disk and online as well. What most of these materials have in common is the fundamental truth that if you cannot read, you cannot get at the ideas held there.

The estimates of illiteracy in the United States range from 15 to 50 percent, in large part because no one has come up with a universally acceptable definition of illiteracy. Are you literate if you can fill out a job application? Or understand a daily newspaper? Or follow a lengthy, reasoned piece in a textbook? No matter what the figure, the Venetian byways of online information are closed if you cannot read. A newspaper reviewer I recently came across wondered what the use of an information highway was if half the population could not read.

Libraries stand at the place in society where the Word lives: where information, reading, the basic tools, and the electronic future meet in a place that belongs to all the people.

Our mission includes, then, a deep commitment to literacy in all of its forms. Libraries offer that chance and they offer an even better thing: the possibility of finding the truth. We know that anyone can say anything in print, or on the Internet, but that does not make it true. By providing the widest possible areas of coverage, and the guidance to find what our patrons seek, we facilitate their finding what is true for them.

Slaves in pre–Civil War United States were forbidden to learn to read. Carl Sagan wrote in the annual report of the Literacy Volunteers of America, "It was well understood that reading was the ticket to freedom. There are many kinds of slavery and many kinds of freedom, but reading is still the ticket." In presenting a service award to a Bronx, New York, librarian recently, Allison Maher Stern remarked, "Libraries saved my life. Without reading, there is no hope." To help people to read and to search for the truth isn't a bad mission statement.

I always seem to be a couple of years behind on the current street slang, but the kids in the Bronx, as a mark of satisfaction or approval, say, "Word." In school or academic or public libraries, we are in the place to give them the words they need.

WEBSITES

Websites for the National Storytelling Festival and the Storytelling Foundation:

http://www.storytellingfestival.net/history.htm

http://www.storytellingfoundation.com/center.htm

■ BIBLIOGRAPHY ■

This bibliography lists all of the books, articles, and websites cited in the various chapters. Books and articles are grouped together; websites follow.

Books and Articles

Anderson, Jim, and Andrea Lee. "Literacy Teachers Learning a New Literacy: A Study of the Use of Electronic Mail in a Reading Education Class." *Reading Research and Instruction* 34 (spring 1995): 222–38.

Apps, J. W. *Mastering the Teaching of Adults* (Malabar, Fla.: Krieger, 1991).

Baer, V. "Computers as Composition Tools: A Case Study of Student Attitudes." *Journal of Computer-Based Instruction* 15 (1988): 144–48.

Balajthy, Ernest. "The Effects of Teacher Purpose on Achievement Gains." *Reading & Writing Quarterly* 16, no. 3 (July 2000): 289–94.

Beach, R., and D. Lundell. "Early Adolescents' Use of Computer-Mediated Communication in Writing and Reading." In *Handbook of Literacy and Technology: Transformations in a Post-Typographic World.* Mahwah, N.J.: Erlbaum Assoc., 1998.

Beldsoe, Lucy Jane. *Working Parts: A Novel.* Seattle: Seal Press, 1997.

Bell, Resonja (changed to Willoughby). "Education Is the Way Out." In *Oakland Readers.* Oakland, Calif.: Oakland Public Library, 1996.

Bernhardt, S., S. Edwards, and P. Wojahn. "Teaching College Composition with Computers: A Program Evaluation Study." *Written Communication* 6 (1989): 108–33.

Blankenship Cheatham, J. *Tutor: A Collaborative Approach to Literacy Instruction.* Syracuse, N.Y.: Literacy Volunteers of America, 1993.

Brady, L. "Overcoming Resistance: Computers in the Writing Classroom." *Computers and Composition* 7 (1990): 21–33.

Case, C., and D. M. Truscott. "The Lure of Bells and Whistles: Choosing the Best Software to Support Reading Instruction." *Reading & Writing Quarterly* 15 (1999): 361–69.

DuPrey, A. *Maintaining the Balance: A Guide to 50/50 Management.* Syracuse, N.Y.: Literacy Volunteers of America, 1992.

Forman, E. A., and C. B. Cazden. "Exploring Vygotskian Perspectives in Education: The Cognitive Value of Peer Interaction." In *Theoretical Models and Processes of Reading,* 4th ed. Newark, Del.: International Reading Assoc., 1994.

Freire, Paulo. "The Adult Literacy Process as Cultural Action for Freedom." *Harvard Educational Review* 30 (May 1970): 205–25.

_____ *Pedagogy of Hope.* New York: Continuum, 1992.

_____ *Pedagogy of the Oppressed.* New York: Continuum, 1970.

Frey, P. *Litstart: Strategies for Adult Literacy and ESL Tutors.* Okemos, Mich.: Michigan Literacy, 1999.

Giroux, H. *Teachers as Intellectuals: Toward a Critical Pedagogy of Learning.* Critical Education series. Bergin and Garvey, 1988.

Hartman, K., C. Neuwirth, S. Kiesler, L. Sproull, C. Cochran, M. Palmquist, and D. Zubrow. "Patterns of Social Interaction and Learning to Write: Some Effects of Network Technologies." *Written Communication* 8 (1991): 79–113.

Hoyles, C., L. Healy, and R. Sutherland. "Patterns of Discussion between Pupil Pairs in Computer Environments and Non-computer Environments." *Journal of Computer Assisted Learning* 7 (1991): 210–28.

Karchmer, R. A. "Understanding Teachers' Perspectives of Internet Use in the Classroom: Implications for Teacher Education and Staff Development." *Reading & Writing Quarterly* 16 (2000): 81–85.

Labbo, L. D., and D. Reinking. "Negotiating the Multiple Realities of Technology in Literacy Research and Instruction." *Reading Research Quarterly* 35 (1999): 478–92.

Long, Sarah Ann. "Libraries Can Help Build Sustainable Communities." *American Libraries* 31 (June/July 2000): 7.

McDonald, H., and L. Ingvarson. *Free at Last? Teachers, Computers and Independent Learning.* Paper presented at the annual meeting of the American Educational Research Association, San Francisco, Calif., 1995. (ERIC Document Reproduction Service No. ED 389 278)

Mackinson, J. A., and J. K. Peyton. "Interactive Writing on a Computer Network: A Teacher/Researcher Collaboration." In *Delicate Balances:*

Collaborative Research in Language Education. Urbana, Ill.: National Council of Teachers of English, 1993.

Marcum, Deanna B. and Elizabeth W. Stone. "Literacy: The Library Legacy." *American Libraries* (March 1991): 202–05.

Mayher, J. S. *Uncommon Sense.* Portsmouth, N.H.: Boynton/Cook, 1990.

Miller, Larry. "Multimedia and Young Children's Symbol Weaving." *Reading & Writing Quarterly* 14 (Jan.-March 1998): 109–14.

Moore, M. "Computers Can Enhance Transactions between Readers and Writers." *Reading Teacher* 42 (1989): 608–11.

Niederhauser, D. S., and T. Stoddart. *Teachers' Perspectives on Computer-Assisted Instruction: Transmission versus Construction of Knowledge.* Paper presented at the annual meeting of the American Educational Research Association, New Orleans, La., 1994. (ERIC Document Reproduction Service No. ED 374 116)

1998 Illinois Statistical Abstract. Bureau of Economic and Business Research. College of Commerce and Business Administration. University of Illinois at Urbana-Champaign.

Papert, Seymour A. *Mindstorms: Children, Computers, and Powerful Ideas.* 2nd ed. New York: Basic Books, 1999.

Planning for Results: A Public Library Transformation Process. Chicago and London: American Library Association, 1999.

Rosenbluth, G., and W. Reed. "The Effects of Writing-Process-Based Instruction and Word Processing on Remedial and Accelerated 11th Graders." *Computers in Human Behavior* 8 (1992): 120–42.

Sanaoui, R, and S. Lapkin. "A Case Study of an ESL Senior Secondary Course Integrating Computer Networking." *Canadian Modern Language Review* 48 (1992): 225–52.

Schement, Jorge Reina, and Terry Curtis. *Tendencies and Tensions of the Information Age.* Somerset, N.J.: Transaction, 1997.

Schwartz, J. "Using an Electronic Network to Play the Scales of Discourse." *English Journal* 79 (1990): 16–24.

Shor, Ira. *Critical Teaching for Social Change.* Chicago and London: University of Chicago Press, 1992.

Spangenberg, Gail. *Even Anchors Need Lifelines.* Washington, D.C.: Center for the Book in the Library of Congress, August 1996.

Spaulding, C., and D. Lake. *Interactive Effects of Computer Network and Student Characteristics on Students' Writing and Collaborating.* Presented at the annual meeting of the American Educational Research Association, Chicago, Ill., April 1991. (ERIC Document Reproduction Service No. ED 329 966)

Strommen, E. F., and B. Lincoln. "Constructivism, Technology, and the Future of Classroom Learning." *Education and Urban Society* 24 (1992): 466–76.

Tao, L., and D. Reinking. "E-mail and Literacy Education." *Reading & Writing Quarterly* 16, no. 2 (April 2000): 169–74.

Toward an Information Bill of Rights and Responsibilities, ed. by Charles M. Firestone and Jorge Reina Schement. Washington, D.C.: Aspen Institute, 1995.

Vygotsky, L. S. *Mind in Society: The Development of Higher Psychological Processes.* (M. Cole, V. John-Steiner, S. Scribner, and E. Souberman, eds.). Cambridge, Mass.: Harvard University Press, 1978.

Watkins, Christine. "Chapter Report: The State Library Scene (Role of State Library Associations in Literacy Campaigns)." *American Libraries* 28 (May 1997): 10.

Wink, Jean. *Critical Pedagogy: Notes from the Real World.* 2nd ed. Reading, Mass.: Addison-Wesley, 1999.

Websites Mentioned

The mission of the American Library Association can be found at
   http://www.ala.org.

National Institute for Literacy
   www.nifl.gov

Adult Literacy Resource Institute
   http://www2.wgbh.org/mbweis/ltc/alri.html

Literacy Assistance Center
   http://www.lacnyc.org

National Storytelling Festival and the Storytelling Foundation
   http://www.storytellingfestival.net/history.htm http://www.
   storytellingfoundation.com/center.htm

The New York Public Library
   http://www.nypl.org/branch; nypl.org/branch/literacy/

■ CONTRIBUTORS ■

Peggy Barber retired August 1, 2000, from her position as associate executive director for communications of the American Library Association. She was an ALA associate director since 1984 and joined the ALA staff in 1969. Barber also was director of ALA's Office for Recruitment, and worked as a reference librarian at the San Francisco Public Library and as a special projects librarian in Orange County, Calif. A Phi Beta Kappa graduate of the University of California at Riverside, she holds an M.L.S. from Rutgers University and is a member of Beta Phi Mu, the national library science honor fraternity. She chaired the National Coalition for Literacy, 1993–95.

Hans Bos is a senior research associate at the San Francisco office of the Manpower Demonstration Research Corporation. He is project director of the Lila Wallace-Reader's Digest Fund Literacy in Libraries Across America persistence study and co-principal investigator in charge of the quantitative research conducted in this study.

Bruce Carmel has been an educator for 20 years. He has worked in many settings including high school, community college, undergraduate, and graduate programs of universities, summer camps, and adult literacy classes, mostly in New York City. He has managed literacy programs, welfare-to-work programs, parenting programs, and youth programs. Just before coming to Queens Borough Public Library, Bruce worked for two years at the Adult Literacy Media Alliance (ALMA) as curriculum director. He has a bachelor's degree from the University of Cincinnati and a master's in English education from New York University, where he is currently a doctoral student in applied linguistics.

Anita Citron is the manager of the Central Adult Learning Center of the Queens Library in New York City. She has been with the ALC for 11 years, beginning as a volunteer tutor. She is currently completing her master's degree in education and technology at Walden University.

Konni Clayton is literacy director at the Robinson Public Library in Robinson, Ill. She has a B.A. in communications and has extensive advertising and marketing experience. Clayton came to the literacy field in 1996 under the Lila Wallace-Reader's Digest Fund grant initiative, Literacy in Libraries across America, as special projects coordinator. After two years in that position, she was promoted to literacy program director. Clayton has written and secured grant funding from the Secretary of State of Illinois, Lila Wallace-Reader's Digest Fund, Mary Heath Foundation, and Claypool Foundation. Clayton is currently working on uncovering and understanding learning barriers of adults by cooperating in a learner persistence initiative.

John Comings is the director of the National Center for the Study of Adult Learning and Literacy (NCSALL) at the Harvard University Graduate School of Education. He is a co-principal investigator in charge of qualitative research conducted in the LILAA persistence study.

Sondra Cuban is a research associate at NCSALL, on the LILAA persistence study qualitative research team. Sondra_cuban@gse.harvard.edu

GraceAnne A. DeCandido is a writer, editor, and teacher for her own company, Blue Roses Consulting. She was born, raised, and educated in the Bronx, New York City, where she still lives (B.A., Fordham University; M.L.S. Columbia University). She spent ten years as a librarian at NYPL, the Parsons School of Design, and NYU, and twelve years in library publishing, working for the Special Libraries Association, *Library Journal, School Library Journal,* and the late, lamented *Wilson Library Bulletin.* She's been a book reviewer for more than 27 years, has published widely in print and on the web on library topics that range from Intranets to Giles on TV's *Buffy the Vampire Slayer.* ladyhawk@well.com; http://www.well.com/user/ladyhawk/gadhome.html

Sherry Drobner has been director of a library-based literacy program since 1988; she comes from a community activist background. She is interested in the power of language and literacy, particularly how both are used to construct social barriers. She is currently a graduate student at University of California, Berkeley, researching the impact of school-based literacies on family life. SDrobner@aclibrary.org

Kathy Endaya, Project READ director, has 13 years of experience in library literacy. In 1988 she joined the Redwood City Project READ staff and has been the director since 1994. Initially a library-based one-on-one adult literacy program, Project READ now extends services to adults, parents, and school-aged children in a variety of different settings including schools, Boys & Girls Clubs, correctional facilities, and library settings. With the goal of a literate Redwood City community by the year 2020, Endaya is passionate about a student-centered, intergenerational approach, and the program's commitment to fueling the fire of hope through literacy in her community.

Decklan Fox was born in Trinidad, West Indies, and emigrated to New York in June 1980. He attended York College of the City University of New York and graduated with a B.S. in information systems management He holds graduate degrees in English education, language, and literacy from City College of CUNY, and instructional technology and media from Columbia University, Teachers College. He is currently the literacy education specialist at the New York Public Library. dfox@nypl.org

Martín Gómez is executive director of the Brooklyn Public Library, the nation's fifth-largest library system. He joined Brooklyn Public Library in 1995 and continues his lifelong commitment to encouraging diversity in libraries. Gómez is an elected member of the American Library Association Executive Board. Other memberships include the Board of National Video Resources, Board of Directors of the Brooklyn Chamber of Commerce, the Poets House, and the Regents Commission on Library Services. In 1991 he served as president of REFORMA, the National Association to Promote Library Services for the Spanish Speaking. Gómez is a graduate of the University of California, Los Angeles, where he received a B.A. in English in 1975. He received an M.L.S. from the University of Arizona, Tucson, in 1976.

Deborah Guerra joined the Brooklyn (N.Y.) Public Library Learning Centers in 1990 and worked as education coordinator until 1997. Today she is a part-time tutor trainer. She earned her M. A. degree in remedial reading from Teachers College, Columbia University, and was an adult literacy teacher for more than five years before working at the library.

Dale Lipschultz is the literacy officer in the Office for Literacy and Outreach Services of the American Library Association. Her focus is on building ALA's capacity in adult literacy by working with ALA's divisions and offices in Chicago and Washington, D.C., supporting the efforts of library-literacy programs in communities, and collaborating with national partners, government agencies, private funders, and corporate sponsors. Prior to assuming that position, she was the senior program associate with the Illinois Literacy Resource Development Center (ILRDC), where she provided technical assistance to the 13 library literacy programs in ALA's Literacy in Libraries across America Initiative funded by the Lila Wallace-Reader's Digest Fund. She played a leadership role in several Chicago-based literacy initiatives. She was the coordinator of the Read with a Child Literacy Program at La Rabida Children's Hospital and Research Center, the executive director of Reach Out and Read Family Literacy Program (ROAR), and project director of the Literacy and Health Partnership, also in Chicago. She has a Ph.D. in child development from the Erikson Institute in Chicago.

Leslie Eldridge McGinnis is a graduate of the University of Wisconsin-Madison Library School and has been a professional librarian since 1974. She has worked at San Francisco Public Library, Boise Public Library, South San Francisco Public Library, and Oakland Public Library. She has directed Second Start, Oakland Public Library's adult literacy program, since 1989. In 1998 Second Start received the Public Library Association's Advancement of Literacy Award. Its Oakland Readers series is now published by New Readers Press, and a more recent learner-centered curriculum is available through Peppercorn Press.

Carol Morris has been the literacy program director at the Waukegan Public Library since its initial funding in 1985. In early 1986 the Lake County Literacy Program coalition was formed with the library, the College of Lake County (community college), and Literacy Volunteers of Lake County, Inc. as the three partners. An avid computer user, Carol has been one of the major forces behind the library and literacy program's commitment to technology. She has presented at state and national conferences on using computers with adult new readers. Currently, Carol is expanding her computer skills by learning how to develop multimedia projects for adult learners. cmorris@nslsilus.org

Sarah Nixon is an assistant professor of reading at Southwest Missouri State University. She has more than 10 years of experience teaching ABE, GED, and ESL, and working with adult literacy programs. Her Ph.D. dissertation was on the use of computer technology in literacy education.

Dinah L. O'Brien, director of the Plymouth Public Library, Plymouth, Massachusetts, received a B.S. in library science from Madison College in Harrisonburg, Virginia, in 1972, and an M.L.S. from the University of Rhode Island in 1984. She has been an elementary/middle school librarian, an academic librarian, and director of two public libraries in Massachusetts. She is an active member of the American Library Association and the Public Library Association, serving on the PLA Intellectual Freedom Committee and chairing the Public Library Systems Committee. She is currently cochair of the Massachusetts Library Association Conference Committee. In Plymouth, she has been responsible for treating the Literacy Department as a full library department, and securing funding through municipal appropriation.

Susan K. O'Connor is the literacy program manager in the Brooklyn (N.Y.) Public Library and a librarian. The literacy program comprises six technology-rich learning centers serving 700 adult new readers and two facilities in the Brooklyn House of Detention for Men. O'Connor spearheaded the publishing of the *Technology Toolkit* in 1999 and is editor in chief of the quarterly *TechTalk*. She holds a B.A. in psychology from CCNY and a M.L.S. from Pratt Institute.

Satia Marshall Orange is director of the Office for Literacy and Outreach Services of the American Library Association. Her office serves as the liaison for the OLOS Advisory Committee with three subcommittees on library services to poor and homeless people, American Indians, and intergenerational groups; three roundtables; the Literacy Assembly; and five associations of librarians of color. Her work addresses equity of access to information in libraries, one of ALA's five key action areas, and the dissemination of information and resources to librarians serving underserved and underrepresented populations in library communities.

Tim Ponder is a technology consultant with six years of experience in offering computer support to adult education programs and initiatives. Technology training, planning, implementation, software review, and web design are areas of special interest. Tim has worked with the National Institute for Literacy, Literacy Volunteers of America, the American Library Association, Laubach Literacy, and others at the local, state, and national levels. tponder@zhost.net

Lynne A. Price is literacy instruction supervisor for Project READ, San Francisco. She also teaches small-group classes, facilitates tutor-training classes, schedules tutor continuing education workshops and learner classes, and is responsible for Project READ book collection development. She has a B.A. in education, and is working to complete an M.A. in education.

Gary E. Strong has served as the director of the Queens Library since September 1994. The Queens Library is the largest circulating library system in the country, reaching a record circulation level of 17 million items and 16 million library visits in the fiscal year ending June 30, 1999. His career spans more than 30 years as a librarian and library administrator. Before coming to Queens, he was the state librarian of California from 1980 to 1994. He was a founder and member of the Board of Directors of the California State Library Foundation, and is now a director emeritus of that body. Prior to that he spent four years with the Washington State Library system as deputy state librarian (1979–1980) and associate director for services (1976–1979). gstrong@queenslibrary.org.

Lou Saunders Sua is the branch manager at the V. H. Chavis Lifelong Learning Branch Library of the Greensboro Public Library in Greensboro, North Carolina. Lou has worked in libraries for 23 years, starting in children's work in 1977 after the birth of her first child. She has been involved in literacy, leadership, and empowerment training since 1990. lou.sua@ci.greensboro.nc.us

Steve Sumerford is assistant director of the Greensboro Public Library. He is a cofounder of the Community of Readers and has been involved with literacy work for 15 years. He can be reached at steve.sumerford@ci.greensboro.nc.us